Ten Life Histories

Ten Life Histories

Berlin Prostitutes and the Sexual Question,
by Wilhelm Hammer

Stephen Carruthers and Jill Suzanne Smith (eds)

Peter Lang
Oxford · Bern · Berlin · Bruxelles · New York · Wien

Bibliographic information published by Die Deutsche Nationalbibliothek.
Die Deutsche Nationalbibliothek lists this publication in the Deutsche Nationalbibliografie;
detailed bibliographic data is available on the Internet at http://dnb.d-nb.de.

A catalogue record for this book is available from the British Library.

Library of Congress Cataloging-in-Publication Data

Names: Smith, Jill Suzanne, 1972- editor. | Carruthers, Stephen, 1956- editor.
Title: Ten life histories : Berlin prostitutes and the sexual question, by
    Wilhelm Hammer / edited by Jill Suzanne Smith and Stephen Carruthers.
Other titles: Zehn Lebensleàufe Berliner Kontollmèadchen und zehn Beitrèage
    zur Behandlung der geschlechtlichen Frage. English
Description: New York : Peter Lang, 2023. | "Original work by Dr. Wilhelm
    Hammer. Translated from the German by Stephen Carruthers. Co-edited by
    Jill Suzanne Smith and Stephen Carruthers"--Provided by publisher. |
    Includes bibliographical references and index.
Identifiers: LCCN 2022040275 (print) | LCCN 2022040274 (ebook) | ISBN
    9781800796973 (paperback) | ISBN 9781800796980 (ebook) | ISBN
    9781800796997 (epub) | ISBN 9781800796997 q(epub) | ISBN
    9781800796980 q(ebook) | ISBN 9781800796973 q(paperback)
Subjects: LCSH: Prostitutes--Germany--Berlin--Biography. |
    Prostitution--Germany--Berlin--History. | Women--Germany--Berlin--Social
    conditions.
Classification: LCC HQ200.B4 Z93 2023 (ebook) | LCC HQ200.B4 (print) | DDC
    306.74/0943155 23/eng/20221--dc21
LC record available at https://lccn.loc.gov/2022040275

Cover image: Heinrich Zille, *In der Kaschemme* (ca. 1910). Wikimedia Commons. In the
public domain.
Cover design by Brian Melville for Peter Lang.

ISBN 978-1-80079-697-3 (print)
ISBN 978-1-80079-698-0 (ePDF)
ISBN 978-1-80079-699-7 (ePUB)

© Peter Lang Group AG 2023

Published by Peter Lang Ltd, International Academic Publishers,
Oxford, United Kingdom
oxford@peterlang.com, www.peterlang.com

Stephen Carruthers and Jill Suzanne Smith have asserted their right under the Copyright,
Designs and Patents Act, 1988, to be identified as Editors of this Work.

All rights reserved.

All parts of this publication are protected by copyright.
Any utilisation outside the strict limits of the copyright law, without the permission of the
publisher, is forbidden and liable to prosecution.
This applies in particular to reproductions, translations, microfilming, and storage and processing
in electronic retrieval systems.

This publication has been peer reviewed.

Contents

Acknowledgements	vii
Preface	ix
Translator's Note	xix
Ten Life Histories	1
Glossary	91
Notes on Contributors	95

Acknowledgements

Translator's Acknowledgements

Firstly, I would like to thank Jill Suzanne Smith for kindly agreeing to write a preface to Dr. Hammer's text. The translator would also like to acknowledge the contribution of Dietmar Jazbinsek in his ground-breaking article, "Lebensgeschichte und Eigensinn: Über die Biographie und die Biographieforschung des Dirnenarztes Wilhelm Hammer," about the life and work of Dr. Hammer in the journal *Mitteilung der Magnus-Hirschfeld-Gesellschaft* published by the Magnus-Hirschfeld-Gesellschaft. I would also like to thank Dr. Deirdre McGowan for her review of the translation and helpful suggestions. I would also like to acknowledge the valuable comments of three anonymous reviewers of this translation and my translator's note. Finally, I would like to acknowledge the unstinting encouragement and invaluable assistance of Laurel Plapp, commissioning editor at Peter Lang, in making this publication possible.

Co-editor's Acknowledgements

Jill Suzanne Smith gives her sincerest thanks to Stephen Carruthers and Laurel Plapp for inviting her to be part of this important project, one that reveals the complexity of turn-of-the-century discourses on prostitution in Berlin. She is grateful to her family for offering support and showing patience as she took on yet another writing project. And finally, she dedicates her Preface to the Bowdoin College students in her course "Making

Sex a Science: Sexology and Its Representations from Krafft-Ebing to Kinsey," in the spring semester of 2022, whose incisive and lively discussions of Foucault, Hirschfeld and Krafft-Ebing inspired and shaped her own critical framing of Hammer's work.

JILL SUZANNE SMITH

Preface

True Confessions?

Before she became a registered prostitute in Berlin, the Catholic-born "Elsa Streng" worked as a governess in Paris, travelled around western Europe with a Baron, had a handful of casual affairs and had intercourse with men – some wealthy, some not – for money. After returning to Berlin at the end of one affair, she found herself seeking shelter in a home for wayward girls. There she was given a list of addresses, but "Elsa made no use of the addresses, since she would not enter a catholic girl's home, because there she would have to confess, and *she wouldn't confess*. She preferred prostitution and was arrested in the evening, taken to Alexanderplatz, examined by the resident medical assistant and found to be healthy."[1] Elsa resisted the act of religious confession, perhaps because she did not see her behaviour as sinful, and yet, we readers can assume, confess she did, once she was no longer healthy and found herself in the care of Dr. Wilhelm Hammer. The text that we have before us, translated into English for the first time by Stephen Carruthers, is in part a collection of confessions or "life histories" of registered prostitutes that were requested and written down by Hammer, a medical doctor who specialised in the treatment of venereal diseases. As Hammer himself emphatically claimed, he sought to document his patients' lives without contempt, without "demeaning" them, and above all, he sought the truth. He assured those who told their

---

1   Wilhelm Hammer, *Ten Life Histories of Berlin Prostitutes under Police Control and Ten Contributions to the Management of the Sexual Question*, translated and annotated by Stephen Carruthers, Peter Lang, 2023, at p. 52. Emphasis added.

stories: "You are not required to answer my questions. On one matter I insist. If you give me information, please tell me the truth[.]"[2] But what does it mean to tell the truth about prostitution? How much of the truth is revealed or confessed by the women whose lives are documented here, and how much of it is produced, through the process of interpretation, and judgment of their words, by the doctor himself?

Dr. Wilhelm Hammer's *Ten Life Histories of Berlin Prostitutes* was written and published in 1905, at a time when attempts to discover the truth behind human sexual behaviour were at their height, particularly in German-speaking Europe.[3] In the imperial capital of Berlin, where Germany's rapid industrialisation and urbanisation were felt most acutely, the final decades of the nineteenth century were ones of increasing secularisation and social unmooring. Traditional kinship ties no longer held young men and women in one place; the need for employment and the will to experience life for themselves drew them to the metropole. By 1905 Berlin was the fourth largest city in Europe and both a renowned centre for scientific research and a well-known destination for sex tourism and erotic entertainment.[4] Through the pioneering work of scientists like Iwan Bloch and Magnus Hirschfeld, turn-of-the-century Berlin became the centre for the burgeoning field of sexology, the scientific exploration of human sexuality, and this exploration of sexuality often accompanied sociopolitical activism. Hirschfeld's activism, for example, was aimed at the repeal of Paragraph 175 of the Imperial Criminal Code, which defined male homosexuality as a criminal offense. But Hirschfeld and those in his circle, including dermatologists like Hammer, openly criticised other forms of state regulation of

---

2   Hammer, *supra*, at p. 14.
3   For the sexual question in Germany, Austria and Switzerland see Edward Ross Dickinson, *Sex, Freedom, and Power in Imperial Germany 1880–1914*, Cambridge UP, 2014; Katie Sutton, *Sex between Body and Mind: Psychoanalysis and Sexology in the German-Speaking World, 1890s–1930s*, U of Michigan P, 2019; and Robert Deam Tobin, *Peripheral Desires: The German Discovery of Sex*, U of Pennsylvania P, 2015.
4   See for a portrait of Berlin around the turn of the twentieth century Jill Suzanne Smith, *Berlin Coquette: Prostitution and the New German Woman, 1890–1933*, Cornell UP, 2013, at pp. 3–8.

sexuality, including the system of regulated prostitution and its purported protections against venereal disease. As scientists, they attempted to wrest power and authority over sexual matters from the state and place them in the hands of the health authorities, and in their perceived roles as healers and counsellors, they invited and recorded the confessions of those who sought out or were placed in their care.[5]

Readers of Michel Foucault's *History of Sexuality* will be aware of the power dynamics inherent in the confession and of the role that the confession played in the nineteenth-century European creation of *"scientia sexualis."*[6] The idea that the person who confesses reveals a fully formed truth about sexuality is an illusion, according to Foucault, and the freedom that supposedly comes from confessing is a ruse. For it is the listener to the confession, in this case the doctor or scientist, who has the power to interpret the truth and allow it to be "scientifically validated."[7] As readers of Hammer's *Ten Life Histories*, therefore, we should keep Foucault's words in mind: "the revelation of the confession had to be coupled with the decipherment of what it said. The one who listened was not simply the forgiving master, the judge who condemned or acquitted; he was the master of truth."[8] The truth of prostitution, therefore, is not something that Hammer passively received or objectively observed from the women he interviewed; it is something he drew out of them with questions and something he *produced* through his presentation and analysis of their answers, and he did so from a position of gendered and classed power.

5   On Bloch and Hirschfeld see Sutton, *supra*, at pp. 60–75. See for Hirschfeld also Heike Bauer, *The Hirschfeld Archives: Violence, Death, and Modern Queer Culture*, Temple UP, 2017; Ralf Dose, *Magnus Hirschfeld: The Origins of the Gay Liberation Movement*, translated by Edward H. Willis, Monthly Review Press, 2014; and Rainer Herrn, Michael Thomas Taylor, and Annette F. Timm, "Magnus Hirschfeld's Institute for Sexual Science: A Visual Sourcebook," in *Not Straight from Germany: Sexual Publics and Sexual Citizenship since Magnus Hirschfeld*, edited by Taylor, Timm, and Herrn, U of Michigan P, 2017, at pp. 37–79.
6   Michel Foucault, *The History of Sexuality: Volume 1: An Introduction*, translated by Robert Hurley, 1978, reprinted by Vintage, 1990, at p. 58. Italics in original.
7   Foucault, *supra*, at p. 66.
8   Foucault, *supra*, at pp. 66–67.

Sexological Case Studies and the Negotiation of Power

As important as it is for us to be cognisant of Hammer's privileged position in terms of class and gender, it is equally important to see the women, or "girls," as he called them, as individuals whose stories exist in tension with the doctor's interpretive narrative. In that tension lies a modicum of agency, of disruption, of negotiation. Historians of queer sexualities have in recent years encouraged us to think both "with and beyond Foucault" in order to see both the oppressive and emancipatory potential in the ways that so-called deviant sex was written about in the late nineteenth- and early twentieth centuries.[9] As perceived sexual deviants themselves, prostitutes were often viewed by sexologists as objects of study. Indeed, because Hammer's text is one that, at least in part, seeks to explain prostitution to its readers, posing questions of which aspects of a registered prostitute's personality are congenital and which are acquired, it should be read in the context of the sexological case studies of sexual deviance presented by Richard von Krafft-Ebing in his monumental work *Psychopathia Sexualis*, the final edition of which appeared just after the author's death in 1903.[10] Between the book's initial publication in 1886 and its last edition, Krafft-Ebing substantially revised *Psychopathia Sexualis*, adding new case studies to it and including first-person narratives written by self-professed "perverts" who often pushed back against Krafft-Ebing's descriptions or diagnoses of sexual pathologies.[11] In their investigation of the case study as

---

9   See Sutton, *supra*, at pp. 14–16, and Scott Spector, "Introduction. After *The History of Sexuality*? Periodicities, Subjectivities, Ethics," in *After "The History of Sexuality"? German Genealogies with and beyond Foucault*, edited by Scott Spector, Helmut Puff, and Dagmar Herzog, Berghahn Books, 2012, at p. 6.

10 Richard von Krafft-Ebing, *Psychopathia Sexualis*, translated by Franklin S. Klaf, Arcade, 1965.

11 Harry Oosterhuis argues that in order to understand how sexual perversions were constructed, "it is necessary to enter the subjective world of individuals who read Krafft-Ebing's work and responded to it, and to take their intentions, purposes, and meanings seriously on their own terms." See Oosterhuis, "Richard von Krafft-Ebing's 'Step-Children of Nature': Psychiatry and the Making of Homosexual

one of the key scientific and literary genres of the fin-de-siècle, Birgit Lang, Joy Damousi, and Alison Lewis emphasise the "'slippery' quality of the genre," and argue that "case studies regularly became sites of reinterpretation and translation, sometimes of resistance."[12] Following the lead of these scholars, readers of Hammer's text should recognise it as a slippery, confusing text with multiple points of disjunction between the doctor's explanatory narrative and the life histories of the prostitutes. The moments of contradiction draw our attention, and because they unnerve us, they invite closer analysis.

In both style and content, Hammer's work is rife with contradictions. The narrative of Hammer's *Ten Life Histories* vacillates, often quite jarringly, between the more casual, colloquial first-person stories of the "girls" and Hammer's third-person exposition, which is itself inconsistent in style. At times it reads like a list of family maladies or squandered job opportunities, and at others it poses questions; at the end of each life history, it delivers its judgment, its explanation for why each girl was susceptible to prostitution. Some girls are lazy (Anna Schlaff, Dorothea Schwächlich), some hail from morally lax homes (Christine Leichtfuss) or were corrupted by permissive environments (Berta Wirt) and some are constitutionally sensual (Elsa Streng, Klara Rache) or even criminal (Frida Schlecht). We can detect the influence of Krafft-Ebing's work on Hammer, particularly the tendency to pathologise his patients. In the cases of Christine Leichtfuss and Klara Rache, for instance, the former is described by the doctor as overly sensual and vain, suffering from "a serious innate hindrance," while the latter is a potential sadist with "the desire to subjugate men."[13] Sadism was considered quite rare, and hence pathological, for women in the sexual norms laid out by Krafft-Ebing, who insisted that female sexuality was naturally passive.[14] Indeed we can detect a clear pattern in Hammer's text when it comes to active female sexuality: when it appears in the form of

---

Identity," in *Science and Homosexualities*, edited by Vernon A. Rosario, Routledge, 1997, pp. 67–88, at p. 70.

12   Birgit Lang, Joy Damousi and Alison Lewis, "Introduction," *A History of the Case Study: Sexology, Psychoanalysis, Literature*, Manchester UP, 2017, at p. 3 and p. 2.
13   Hammer, *supra*, at p. 32 and pp. 87–88.
14   Krafft-Ebing, *supra*, at p. 8 and p. 85.

promiscuity – sex with multiple men, even if not for pay, it is consistently and uncritically conflated with commodified sex.[15] When it appears in the form of masturbation or lesbian desire, it is classified as a sign of depravity or, in the case of Gretchen Früh, a source of "grief."[16] When it comes to real sources of grief, however, such as the deaths of multiple children (in the cases of Berta Wirt and Klara Rache), or physical abuse, rape and incest in the case of Frida Schlecht, Hammer ignores these traumas. But we as readers can ask the question: why is the Lombrosian explanation of an inborn criminal nature the most logical explanation for Frida Schlecht's slide into underage prostitution when there are myriad social factors that speak to her repeated physical degradation by the men and boys in her immediate surroundings?

The girls' stories create moments of tension with Hammer's official narrative, and these tensions open up spaces for alternative readings. Christine Leichtfuss, one of only two native Berliners featured in the text, unabashedly chain smokes when she's "having a good time," and she defiantly contends that she is "a bit reckless, but otherwise not bad." She loves her work as a barmaid and chooses to prostitute herself over entering domestic service.[17] The interspersed quotes by Leichtfuss counter Hammer's assertion that she is morally depraved, and that prostitution is a social misery. Indeed, her resistance to domestic service points to the possibility that prostitution was a line of work that some women chose over other forms of work they deemed to be less favourable, perhaps due to lower pay, perhaps due to class and gender structures that made them demeaning. For other women, like Anna Schlaff, whose first-person narrative is the most extensive of the life histories and who came from a family of servants, domestic service to the upper class was a means to travel, luxury and adventure. When read in combination with the histories of Elsa Streng, who sought work in Paris

---

15   See especially the cases of Elsa Streng, in which Hammer claims "Elsa readily engaged in prostitution, even when she was not paid;" Frida Schlecht; Gretchen Früh; and Klara Rache. Hammer, *supra*, at pp. 54, 60–61, 67, 85–86.

16   Hammer, *supra*, at p. 67. On masturbation in the text, see Hammer, *supra*, at pp. 31, 33, 67, 74, 87; on lesbianism, see Hammer, *supra*, at pp. 31, 33, 61–62, 74, 87. Note that these two phenomena are, more often than not, discussed on the same pages.

17   Hammer, *supra*, at pp. 34–35.

and Berlin out of a desire to escape provincial life, and Hulda Schnell, who admits that she fell into prostitution out of boredom and curiosity, we can read these women's narratives not only against the grain of Hammer's interpretation of their lives, but also against existing scholarship on this text that defines the prostitutes' "Reizhunger" as exclusively sexual. After all, the German term "Reiz" is not just about stimulation but about allure, and the allure of the big city of Berlin was often just as much about adventure and social experimentation as it was about sexuality.[18]

Documents of Urban Life

Unlike Richard von Krafft-Ebing's *Psychopathia Sexualis*, Hammer's study was not marketed as a scientific text; rather, it was published in a series of affordable pamphlets pitched to a mass audience – Hans Ostwald's *Großstadt-Dokumente*. Ostwald (1873–1940) is perhaps best described as an urban ethnographer. His multivolume studies of prostitution, the sexual underworld and the demimonde in Berlin include the *Großstadt-Dokumente* (1904–08), a forty-volume series that he edited and partially authored; *Das Berliner Dirnentum* (*Prostitutes of Berlin*, 1907); and several versions of his *Kultur- und Sittengeschichte Berlins* (*Cultural and Moral History of Berlin*, 1911, 1924, 1926). These studies tell of hierarchies among prostitutes, of secret terms and nicknames, and describe in minute detail the many districts and locales in which readers could experience this world for themselves. Ostwald's books literally map out the world of Berlin prostitution by listing the streets and squares traversed by unregistered prostitutes and providing narrative accounts of men's visits – including his own – to various dance halls and cafés, at

---

18   Dietmar Jazbinsek, "Lebensgeschichte und Eigensinn: Über die Biographie und die Biographieforschung des Dirnenarztes Wilhelm Hammer," *Mitteilungen der Magnus-Hirschfeld-Gesellschaft*, no. 37/38, 2007, pp. 32–61, at p. 34. See also Carruthers's Translator's Note below.

which prostitutes were either employed or conspicuously present.[19] Seen in the context of Ostwald's larger project of documenting urban nightlife and non-normative sexual and gender identities (Hirschfeld wrote one of the first volumes of the *Großstadt-Dokumente* entitled *Berlin's Third Sex*), Hammer's detailed discussions of entertainment establishments (*Damenkneipen*, dance halls), his reprinting of the rules and regulations that constrained the lives of registered prostitutes, and his explicit mention of particular streets and squares allow us to read his work as a sociohistorical document of turn-of-the-century Berlin.

But if we view Hammer's work as a historical document, what do we learn about Berlin's registered prostitutes? When we read Hammer's *Ten Life Histories* alongside archival sources and the meticulous research of historians like Julia Roos, we find demographic patterns regarding the women's social backgrounds to be fairly consistent with historical sources. The majority of the women are young (only two are over the age of 30) and hail from cities or towns other than Berlin. The class backgrounds of their families are primarily petit bourgeois, with artisans, tradesman, low-ranking civil servants and service workers most heavily represented, and the women's own occupational histories show a clear connection between work as domestic servants and registered prostitutes.[20] Again, the trajectories of Anna Schlaff and Elsa Streng reveal the assumption of female servants' sexual availability by their (male) employers, assumptions that often ended in

---

19   Ostwald's works have received renewed attention, both scholarly and popular, with reprints of his 1926 *Berliner Kultur- und Sittengeschichte* (Voltmedia, 2006) available in Berlin bookstores. See for scholarship on Ostwald, Richard J. Evans, *Tales from the German Underworld*, Yale UP, 1998, at pp. 171–193; Peter Fritzsche, "Vagabond in the Fugitive City: Hans Ostwald, Imperial Berlin, and the *Großstadtdokumente*," *Journal of Contemporary History*, vol. 29, 1994, at pp. 385–402; Julia Roos, *Weimar Through the Lens of Gender: Prostitution Reform, Woman's Emancipation, and German Democracy, 1919–33*, U of Michigan P, 2010, at pp. 64–66; Dorothy Rowe, *Representing Berlin: Sexuality and the City in Imperial and Weimar Germany*, Ashgate, 2003, at pp. 90–122; and Ralf Thies, *Ethnograph des dunklen Berlins: Hans Ostwald und die Großstadtdokumente 1904–1908*, Böhlau, 2006.

20   See for statistical profiles of Berlin's registered prostitutes Roos, *supra*, at pp. 69–76. See for a similar portrait of prostitutes in Leipzig Victoria Harris, *Selling Sex in the Reich: Prostitutes in German Society, 1914–1945*, Oxford UP, 2010, at pp. 44–55.

forced sexual intercourse, and Christine Leichtfuss's vehement rejection of domestic service points to the exploitative nature of that work. Hammer, however, shows little concern for the economic and sexual exploitation of the women he studies. His concern lies elsewhere and aligns with the assumed male readership of Ostwald's *Großstadt-Dokumente*; from time to time he offers clear warnings to those men who might seek sexual adventure in the German capital. Let us take Hammer's not-so-brief excursion into Berta Wirt's world of the *Damenkneipen* as an example. Berta Wirt, he tells readers, "takes pleasure in the exploitation of men." After delivering his specific character analysis of Berta, Hammer begins to generalise about the *Damenkneipe* and its milieu. At the end of the night, after the *Damenkneipen* like Berta's close, "[t]he waitresses go with a selected client to a café, where they let themselves be entertained. Occasionally, the client can afford the pleasure of spending the night with the girl, with the risk that he might be robbed or catch gonorrhoea as a souvenir of his 'amusement.'"[21] Despite Hammer's repeated contention that he has kept his study free of moralising views of prostitutes, he perpetuates negative stereotypes of prostitutes as petty criminals (here: thieves) and spreaders of venereal disease.

It is with the spread of venereal disease that we arrive at the impetus for – even the truth of – Hammer's project: this is a text that promotes the idea of healthy sex and warns of the dangers of promiscuity. This is a text that openly criticises the state regulation of prostitution as a failed project, both in terms of public health and moral discipline. The vice police, Hammer states in no uncertain terms, make criminals out of wayward women, and in doing so they reinforce the moral prejudices of their time. Hammer's calls for the decriminalisation and deregulation of prostitution, along with his claims that sexual intercourse can be practiced, albeit in moderation, outside the institution of marriage, allow us to view his work alongside that of the social reformers of his day, including radical feminists like Helene Stöcker. Stöcker imagined, much like Hammer does at the very end of his text, a "new morality" for both men and women, one that

---

21 Hammer, *supra*, at pp. 18–19. See for Hammer's insistence that he is not delivering readers portraits of prostitutes as morally depraved, *supra*, at p. 13.

saw sexual abstinence as potentially damaging and opened up possibilities for the sexual fulfilment of both women and men.[22] The critique of abstinence, however, was not an invitation to promiscuity, nor were the calls for prostitution's decriminalisation to be understood as calls for its complete deregulation. Just as Hammer's work foretells the eventual decriminalisation of prostitution in 1927, under the *Reichsgesetz zur Bekämpfung der Geschlechtskrankheiten* (Law to Combat Venereal Diseases), it also foretells the continued surveillance and control of sexually promiscuous women and their bodies. Authority over their bodies shifted from that of the vice police to that of health officials.[23] Venereal disease prevention and the health of the nation remained a top priority in Germany, and because prostitutes and promiscuous women – often seen as one and the same – were seen as uncontested spreaders of disease, their social and sexual autonomy and their human dignity were often sacrificed. That is, perhaps, the clearest truth about prostitution that we can glean from Hammer's text.

Jill Suzanne Smith
Brunswick, Maine, USA

---

22 On sexual intercourse outside of marriage and on the potential of moral reform, see Hammer, *supra*, at pp. 43–47 and at pp. 68–69. On Helene Stöcker's "new morality" and her perspectives on abstinence, prostitution and venereal disease, see Smith, *supra*, at pp. 85–92.

23 See for the *Reichsgesetz zur Bekämpfung der Geschlechtskrankheiten* (RGBG) Roos, *supra*, at pp. 1–3, 10, 90–96, 113, 160–162; Smith, *supra*, at pp. 153–157; and Annette Timm, *The Politics of Fertility in Twentieth-Century Berlin*, Cambridge UP, 2010, at pp. 58–65.

Translator's Note

The primary purpose of this translation is to bring to an English-speaking readership a significant[1] historical document on the regulation and treatment of persons in prostitution[2] in Berlin at the beginning of the twentieth century. Dr. Wilhelm Hammer (1879–1940(?)) provides a record based on interviews of the life histories of ten women under the control of the vice police in Berlin who attended the Women's Hospital Ward at the Berlin Municipal Homeless Shelter in Fröbelstraße where Dr. Hammer

1 See for critical engagement with Dr. Hammer's work: Dietmar Jazbinsek, "Lebensgeschichte und Eigensinn: Über die Biographie und die Biographieforschung des Dirnenarztes Wilhelm Hammer." *Mitteilungen der Magnus Hirschfeld-Gesellschaft*, no. 37/38, 2007, pp. 32–61; Jill Suzanne Smith, *Berlin Coquette: Prostitution and the New German Woman, 1890–1933*, Cornell UP, 2013, at pp. 66–69; and Daniela Sandner, *Konstruierte Männlichkeit*, Bamberg, 2019, *passim*. Subsequent prostitution policies in Germany during the Weimar Republic and the Nazi Germany periods are analysed by Julia Roos in *Weimar through the Lens of Gender: Prostitution Reform, Women's Emancipation, and German Democracy, 1919–1933*, U of Michigan Press, 2010; and "Backlash against Prostitutes' Rights: Origins and Dynamics of Nazi Prostitution Policies." *Journal of the History of Sexuality*, vol. 11, no. 1/2, 2002, pp. 67–94. *JSTOR*, <www.jstor.org/stable/3704552>. Studies on the present-day regulation of prostitution in Germany under the 2002 Prostitution Law include: *Das Prostitutionsgesetz und seine Umsetzung* by Ina Hunecke, Verlag Dr. Kovač, 2011.

2 Current scholarship is divided in its terminology in referring to persons in prostitution. The terms "sex worker," "prostitute," or "prostituted persons" or "prostituted people" are variously adopted in current academic literature, depending on the author's views on prostitution. For a discussion of this divide, see Jane Scoular, *The Subject of Prostitution: Sex Work, Law and Social Theory*, Routledge, 2016, pp. 1–3; and Eilis Ward and Gillian Wylie, "Introduction," in *Feminism, Prostitution and the State: The Politics of Neo-Abolitionism*, Routledge, 2017, pp. 1–11. In this translation, I have used the term "prostitute" on the basis this is the translation given in the leading German-English dictionaries for the terms "Dirne" and "Prostituierte," which are the terms employed by Hammer to refer to a person in prostitution (see Glossary).

worked from 1904 as a physician treating venereal disease.³ He also provides his own analysis of contemporary issues related to prostitution in ten brief articles entitled "Lebenserfahrungen" (Life Lessons). While, as discussed further below, Dr. Hammer's research methodology and the conclusions he draws from his interviews are problematic, and indeed severely criticised by some of his contemporaries,⁴ his research nonetheless supplements the sources available to historians of prostitution in this period, notably contemporary governmental archival records, autobiographies and memoirs.⁵

Prostitution policies, and more generally issues of sexual hygiene and control, were the subject of intense academic and political debate during the Wilhelmine period.⁶ Magnus Hirschfeld (1868–1935), the noted sexologist, and Hans Ostwald (1873–1940), the editor of the *Großstadt-Dokumente*, were members of the Scientific-Humanitarian Committee (*Wissenschaftlich-humanitäres Komitee*) set up by Hirschfeld in 1897 to repeal the section of the German penal code that criminalised homosexuality, in which circle

---

3   Exact dates for the length of Dr. Hammer's residency at the Fröbelstraße are uncertain, but he probably started in 1904. See Manfred Herzel, "Wilhelm Hammer," *Personenlexicon der Sexual-Forschung*, edited by Volkmar Sigusch and Günter Grau, Campus Verlag, 2009, pp. 257–259.

4   Jazbinsek, *supra*, at pp. 36–38.

5   On the use of archives and other sources in prostitution research, and an analysis of some of the difficulties presented in their use, see: Timothy J. Gilfoyle, "Prostitutes in the Archives: Problems and Possibilities in Documenting the History of Sexuality." *The American Archivist*, vol. 57, no. 3, 1994, pp. 514–527. *JSTOR*, <www.jstor.org/stable/40293850>. For a discussion of contemporary autobiographies, and notably the *succès de scandale* of Margarete Böhme's *Tagebuch einer Velorenenen*, published in 1905 and the memoir of Josephine Mutzenbacher, *Die Lebensgeschichte eine wienerischen Dirnen, von selbst erzählt*, published in 1906, see: Dietmar Jazbinsek, *supra*, pp. 41–45.

6   For a detailed historical study of the regulation of prostitution in Berlin in the pre-Wilhelmine Empire, see Kurt Wolzendorff, "Polizei und Prostitution. Eine Studie." *Zeitschrift für die Gesamte Staatswissenschaft / Journal of Institutional and Theoretical Economics*, vol. 67, no. 2, 1911, pp. 218–266, at pp. 225–238. *JSTOR*, <www.jstor.org/stable/40743661>.

Dr. Hammer was a guest.⁷ Other notable contemporaries of Dr. Hammer who published on prostitution were the sociologist Georg Simmel (1858–1918), the sexologist Iwan Bloch (1872–1922) and the artist Heinrich Zille (1858–1929).⁸

Dr. Hammer wrote *Zehn Lebensläufe Berliner Kontollmädchen und zehn Beiträge zur Behandlung der geschlechtlichen Frage* (Ten Life Histories of Berlin Prostitutes under Police Control and Ten Contributions to the Management of the Sexual Question) as a contribution to the *Großstadt-Dokumente*. This was a sociological work in fifty volumes edited by Hans Ostwald and published between 1904 and 1908 which documents the full variety of life in Berlin and other big cities, including Vienna and Hamburg.⁹ Dr. Hammer made a further contribution to the series, *Die Tribadie Berlins*, published in July 1906, on the theme of lesbianism and also based on a study of ten life histories interspersed with ten commentaries. In 1906, the Berlin District Court ordered the seizure of all copies of *Die Tribadie Berlins*.¹⁰

Dr. Hammer's work, in addition to its contribution to prostitution research, also sheds circumstantial light on aspects of the period of German history beginning with Germany's unification in 1871 into the German Empire under the guidance of Otto von Bismarck (1815–1898),

---

7   Jazbinsek, *supra*, p. 32. Hirschfeld published a chapter "The Origins, Forms, Consequences and Control of Prostitution," in *Die neue Heilmethode*, vol. 4, 1907, pp. 113–120. For a list of Ostwald's numerous publications on prostitution, see Jazbinsek, *supra*, p. 59.

8   Georg Simmel, "Einiges über die Prostitution in Gegenwart und Zukunft." *Schriften zur Philosophie und Soziologie des Geschlechter*, edited by Jürgen Dahme and Klaus Christian Köhnke, Suhrkamp, 1985 (originally published 1892); Iwan Bloch, *Die Prostitution*. vol. 1, *Handbuch der Gesamten Sexualwissenschaft in Einzeldarstellungen*. Louis Marcus, 1912; and Heinrich Zille, *Hurengespäche*, published in 1913 under the pseudonym W. Pfeiffer (see Amanda M. Brian, "Art from the Gutter: Heinrich Zille's Berlin." *Central European History*, vol. 46, no. 1, 2013, pp. 28–60, at p. 60, n. 85. *JSTOR*, <www.jstor.org/stable/43280549>.

9   See: Dietmar Jazbinsek and Ralf Thies, "*Großstadt-Dokumente*". *Metropolenforschung im Berlin der Jahrhundertwende*. <https://bibliothek.wzb.eu/pdf/1996/ii96-501.pdf>.

10 Jazbinsek, *supra*, at p. 52.

and thereafter into the Wilhelmine period from Bismarck's resignation as Chancellor in 1890 until the abdication of Kaiser Wilhelm II (1859–1941) in 1918. While much of Dr. Hammer's focus is on Berlin and Prussia, a number of the women who provided their life histories originated from other states within the German Empire. The life histories provide information about the various categories of primary and secondary of schools at the time, which varied from state to state, and in particular on schools specifically established for the education of girls.[11] In addition, the life histories provide information about the variety of welfare institutes and foundations, both religious and charitable,[12] set up in the period to house and train young women subject to the welfare and penal legislation. The life histories not only exemplify the limited range of work opportunities available to young women at the time, mainly in service or hospitality, but also provides examples where new opportunities were becoming available, as in the life history of Ida Hauptmann.

Dr. Hammer was born in Bad Homburg in the Grand Duchy of Hesse.[13] He trained as a doctor in Freiburg and Berlin but also gained academic qualifications in dentistry, veterinary studies and law. In addition to his work as an assistant physician at the women's ward at the Berlin municipal homeless shelter in the Fröbelstrasse, where he recorded the life histories, Dr. Hammer worked as a doctor in a variety of welfare and penal institutions in Switzerland, Austria, Holland and throughout the German Empire, during which time he updated his research on many of the prostitutes who had given their life histories with the unfulfilled

---

[11] For a historical comparison of the system of education in Prussia and the United States in the nineteenth century, see: Jurgen Herbst, "Nineteenth-Century Schools between Community and State: The Cases of Prussia and the United States." *History of Education Quarterly*, vol. 42, no. 3, 2002, pp. 317–341. *JSTOR*, <www.jstor.org/stable/3217972>.

[12] A repository with a comprehensive list of the numerous state and private welfare institutions for minors operating in Prussia from 1806 to 1936 is available at: *Geheimes Staatsarchiv Preußischer Kulturbesitz. I. HA Rep. 77 B. Ministerium des Innern, Volkswohlfahrt.*

[13] The following biographical information is taken from Dietmar, *supra*, at pp. 56–57. See also: Manfred Herzer, *supra*, at pp. 257–260.

objective of publishing a follow-up study. Dr. Hammer published prolifically in the period 1904–1918, in particular in the journal *Monatsschrift für Harnkrankheiten und sexuelle Hygiene* (Monthly Periodical for Urinary Diseases and Sexual Hygiene), which was edited by Dr. Karl Ries. From 1906 until 1908, Dr. Hammer was editor of the same journal under the revised title, *Monatsschrift für Harnkrankheiten, Psyhcopathia sexualis und sexuelle Hygiene*.[14]

Dr. Hammer held non-conformist and often marginal views on many themes touched upon in *Ten Life Histories*. Most controversially, he concluded that: "prostitutes are not driven onto the streets by hunger"[15] but rather as a result "of their 'Reizhunger', their sexual drive which is unsatisfied in normal life."[16] Dr. Hammer supported this thesis by his contentious analysis of the ten life histories, in particular that of Elsa Streng, and the availability of alternative opportunities to women under police control, as evidenced by information on labour offices and welfare institutes provided by the vice police.[17] This conclusion was questioned by Hans Ostwald in his Introduction to *Ten Life Histories* and severely criticised in the contemporary social-democratic press.[18] A second view, which was also controversial in his time and is in diametric conflict with modern standards, was Dr. Hammer's advocacy of the benefits of corporal punishment, mentioned in the section of the book entitled "Training for Young Prostitutes," but developed more extensively in other writing into a fully-fledged theory of the

---

14 A selection of Dr. Hammer's publications is given by Manfred Herzer, *supra*, at p. 259; and in the works cited list of Jazbinsek, *supra*, at p. 58. See also the list of Dr. Hammer's publications at *Gesamtverzeichnis des deutschsprachigen Schrifftums* (GV), Hilmar Schmuck and Willi Gorzny (eds), K. G. Saur, 1982, at pp. 250–251.
15 *Ten Life Histories*, at p. 89.
16 This quotation is from Jazbinsek, *supra*, at p. 34 (my trans.).
17 *Ten Life Histories*, at p. 54 and p. 89.
18 Jazbinsek, *supra*, at p. 35. It is beyond the scope of this work to examine modern scholarship on the causes and consequences of prostitution. For a valuable overview, see: Ana S. Q. Liberato and Kathleen Ratajczak, "The Feminist Debate on Prostitution and Trafficking: Reflections for a Unified and Theory-Driven Approach." *International Review of Modern Sociology*, vol. 43, no. 1, 2017, pp. 119–135. *JSTOR*, <www.jstor.org/stable/44510057>.

use and abuse of corporal punishment.[19] A third controversial view espoused by Dr. Hammer in *Ten Life Histories* was his argument in Chapter IV (On the Sexual Question) that prostitutes should not be treated as morally reprehensible, since society did not similarly judge male clients. This position aroused the reprobation of feminists, notably Ella Mensch (1859–1935), a leading advocate of women's rights in Berlin, as did his further contention that "respectable women" repressed their sexuality in monogamous marriage.[20] A number of Dr. Hammer's other ideas reflected contemporary, and since discredited, criminological theories, notably those of Cesare Lombroso (1835–1909) on innate criminality, and the use of graphology as a means of character analysis.[21] These controversial views over time resulted in Dr. Hammer's loss of influence and recognition in professional circles.[22] Dr. Hammer, however, expressed progressive views on a number of issues. In Chapter III of *Ten Life Histories* (Training of Young Prostitutes), he advocates improvements in the professional training and education of young women in welfare or penal institutions as a result of engaging in prostitution. In Chapter VI (Criminality and Prostitution) he advocates the decriminalisation of women in prostitution.[23] Dr. Hammer also highlights in Chapter II (The Berlin Vice Police and their Consequences) the ineffectiveness of the regulations and obligatory medical examinations imposed on prostitutes by the Berlin vice control regime, and in Chapter X (Reform Proposals) he recommends the abolition of such controls. Furthermore, in Chapter II (The Berlin Vice Police and their Consequences), Dr. Hammer

---

19   See for reference to these writings and a summary of Dr. Hammer's theories on the appropriate therapeutic gradation of corporal punishment, Jazbinsek, *supra*, at pp. 45–48.

20   See Jazbinsek, *supra*, at pp. 36–37.

21   However, it should be noted that Dr. Hammer in his chapter entitled "Criminality and Prostitution" stated he was unable to verify the Lombrosian theory "that prostitutes are mostly physically degenerated," at p. 64.

22   Jazbinsek, *supra*, at p. 57.

23   A position in contemporary times supported on health grounds by Anand Grover, Special Rapporteur on the right of everyone to the enjoyment of the highest attainable standard of physical and mental health, in a report to the Human Rights Council of 27 April 2010; A/HRC/14/20. See: Section III. Sex Work (pp. 10–14) and Section V. Recommendations (p. 22).

describes the draconian and discriminatory measures that women placed under police control were subjected to, including segregated wards for treatment for venereal diseases in the women's hospital, and advocates for their abolition.

Dr. Hammer's research methodology in *Ten Life Histories* was criticised at the time as unscientific on grounds of the small sample size and the dubious veracity of the selected prostitutes' responses.[24] Dr. Hammer's justification of his research methodology is set out in Chapter I (On Prostitution and Prostitution Research). However, the gathering of reliable statistical information, whether qualitative or quantitative, on prostitution remains to this day problematic.[25]

In this translation, I have provided annotations where I consider a reader may be unfamiliar with a particular reference made by Dr. Hammer, including a specific geographic location, cultural reference or social institution. I have also indicated where there are difficulties in interpreting Dr. Hammer's meaning due to circumlocution or use of obsolete words.

In the footnotes, I have included reference to sources in German where I could not locate a relevant source in English. This is due to the relative paucity of academic material in English on Dr. Hammer and the themes he addresses.[26] I have also included a glossary explaining the meaning of the listed English or German words in the context of Dr. Hammer's usage.

---

24 See Jazbinsek, *supra*, at pp. 40–41. Jazbinsek provides a valuable summary overview in tabular form of 31 women in prostitution whose biographies were published in Dr. Hammer's writings, *supra*, at pp. 60–61.
25 See, H. Wagenaar, "Introduction," *Assessing Prostitution Policies in Europe*, edited by Synnøve Økland Jahnsen and Hendrik Wagenaar, Taylor and Francis, 2018, pp. 1–28, at p. 8.
26 Jill Suzanne Smith discusses *Ten Life Histories* (which she translates as "Ten Biographies of Berlin's Registered Prostitutes") in *Berlin Coquette: Prostitution and the New German Woman, 1890–1933*, *supra*, at pp. 66–69.

Ten Life Histories of Berlin Prostitutes under Police Control
and
Ten Contributions to the Management of the Sexual Question

by

Dr. Wilhelm Hammer (M.D.)
previously Dujour[1]- and First Assistant Physician at the Women's
Hospital Ward at the Berlin Municipal Homeless Shelter
Großstadt Dokumente
Published by Hans Ostwald
Vol. 23

Berlin and Leipzig
Publisher: Hermann Seemann Successor GmbH

---

1   Du Jour: this term is used to describe a system of hospital care by a physician over a 24-hour period, beginning at 8.30 am. During this time, a physician had to remain on-duty. See Daniel Freiberger, "Die Assistenzärzte am Städtischen Krankenhaus Links der Isar bzw. am Klinikum der Medizinischen Fakultät der Universität München im 19. Jahrhundert." Phd. Dissertation, Ludwig-Maximilians-Universität zu München, 2019, at pp. 76–77.

Contents

Introduction ... 5

Life Stories

1. Anna Schlaff ... 7
2. Berta Wirt ... 15
3. Christine Leichtfuss ... 29
4. Dorothea Schwächlich ... 37
5. Elsa Streng ... 49
6. Frida Schlecht ... 59
7. Gretchen Früh ... 65
8. Hulda Schnell ... 71
9. Ida Hauptmann ... 77
10. Klara Rache ... 85

Life Lessons

I. On Prostitution and Prostitution Research ... 12
II. The Berlin Vice Police and Their Consequences ... 19
III. Training of Young Prostitutes ... 33
IV. On the Sexual Question ... 43
V. Remarks on Religion and Sexual Life ... 54
VI. Criminality and Prostitution ... 62
VII. On the Sexual Enlightenment of Adolescents ... 68
VIII. The Male World and Prostitution ... 74
IX. The Benefits and Harms of Prostitution ... 80
X. Reform Proposals ... 88

Introduction

I adopt two approaches to the invitation from the publishers of the *Großstadtdocumente*[1] to make my experiences and observations available to a wider circle of educated readers.

With the ten life stories, described with as much precision as possible, I show the paths that lead to the hospital for prostitutes.

In addition, I address in ten studies important and topical questions in the field that I had the opportunity to study from different perspectives: as house physician at the largest German hospital for prostitutes in Berlin, as prison doctor in a Swiss cantonal punishment institute, and finally as a medical practitioner in the prostitution section of a University town in southern Germany and as medical adviser to a workhouse in Saxony. My material is arranged so that each life history is followed by a study.

The names of the girls have been selected at random so as to spare them any unpleasantness.

As publisher of the *Großstadtdocumente*, I must thank Dr. Hammer for the force and fearlessness with which in this volume he approaches the most sensitive material, the most sensitive issue of modern big city life. It gave me the greatest pleasure that he departs from the customary stereotypes, sets aside dated, insufficient solutions, old prejudices and false, widely-held notions. Only through such qualities can a scholar make a serious contribution to learning. And for this reason, Dr. Hammer has rejected the statistical method. Statistics that only too often forgot the living humans behind the numbers. But Dr. Hammer brings us humanity in its fullness of life, its suffering, its pain and its desire. In this work, he is one of the first to embrace wholeheartedly as comrades the individual, the modern human, everyone who is conscious of their humanity. It has

---

1   *Großstadt-Dokumente* is a work in fifty volumes edited by Hans Ostwald (1873–1940) and published between 1904 and 1908. See: Dietmar Jazbinsek and Ralf Thies. "*Großstadt-Dokumente*". *Metropolenforschung im Berlin der Jahrhundertwende.* <https://bibliothek.wzb.eu/pdf/1996/ii96-501.pdf>.

been from the beginning my endeavour to bring humans closer together. In that I see one of the principal objectives of *Großstadtdocumente*, and indeed the goal of every work which I prize …

I highly value the fact that Dr. Hammer breaks with sentimental stereotypes: only hunger[2] drives the girls onto the streets. It is exactly because he observes and portrays the individual human that he arrives at new conclusions. Thereby, however, he also manages to give each person their due. And it is thus a gratifying fact that as resident physician he got to know in depth hundreds, but hundreds, of street prostitutes and railed against the way in which our modern society treats women whose love is for sale. While certainly he could have from the beginning been tempted to despise the prostitutes — but instead he speaks out strongly in their favour!

A person who is not in agreement in certain respects with the publisher of this volume – there are indeed those who become prostitutes from hunger; and the burden that is imposed by meagre wages on the frail shoulders of young women is also not of a kind to protect sensitive and high-spirited persons from temptation – that person must be pleased that these important questions are treated here with such seriousness and urgency and in a manner that is accessible to the general public. So that is the central subject of interest. First of all come human beings – after them everything else.

Groß-Lichterfelde,[3] June 1905

Hans Ostwald

---

[2] Dr. Hammer's contrarian approach to the role played by hunger in driving women into prostitution is discussed by Jazbinsek, *supra*, at pp. 34–35.

[3] Groß-Lichterfelde was a rural municipality south-west from Berlin: <www.zeno.org/Meyers-1905/A/Gro%C3%9Flichterfelde>.

1 Anna Schlaff

(No. 104 in my files)

She preferred to give me her life history in writing. She writes:

Life History!

I was born in Z. (…) in the year 187(.). At four years old I went with my parents to J. where my father was taken on by Count X. (…), I then lived at my parents' house until my mother died when I was five years old. I then went to a sister of my mother in W. (…) where I stayed until eight years old. I then went to a brother. He had a position with Count A. at castle W. and I stayed there until fourteen years old when I was sent by the Countess to a boarding school in Y., where the Countess paid 240 Marks yearly. I stayed there for two years.

At the boarding school, I trained as a teacher for Sunday schools, kindergartens and young women's associations.[1] I then fell ill with typhus and went to the deaconess house[2] at Y. where I stayed eight months; I then went to Switzerland to recuperate with a woman who was the niece of a female board member of the boarding school by the name of Miss v. T.,[3] where I stayed six weeks; I then returned to Y. and started work at the young women's association, since Miss v. T. was the president of the association.

---

1   For a history of young women's associations (*Jungfrauenvereine*) in this period see, Petra Brinkmeier, *Zur Geschichte des Verbandes der evangelischen Jungfrauenvereine Deutschlands (1890–1918)*, PhD dissertation, U. Potsdam, 2003.
2   See on the founding of deaconess houses (*Diakonissenhause*) in Germany: Emilie G. Briggs, "The Restoration of the Order of Deaconesses." *The Biblical World*, vol. 41, no. 6, 1913, pp. 382–390, at p. 383. *JSTOR*, <www.jstor.org/stable/3142249>.
3   The v. or von (of) was at that period employed in names of the nobility to designate their place of attachment. It is no longer permissible since the abolition of the privileges and titles of rank in 1919, although it may, unlike in Austria, still be incorporated into the person's name. See the judgment of the Court of Justice of the European Union of 2 June 2016: *Bogendorff von Wolffersdorff*, C-438/14.

I stayed there until twenty-six years old. Meanwhile, I spent my holidays here and there and was paid 35 Marks monthly; my first vacation I spent at the villa of the Baroness v. T. at S ... (a Swiss) lake, where at the same time the nephew of the baroness was staying; he took my virginity when I was eighteen years old and paid me 200 Marks. Soon after I suffered from consumption and had to leave work and undergo treatment in the deaconess house; I stayed there eighteen weeks, and then I was transferred to an institute for lung cure[4] in French-speaking Switzerland, where I stayed three weeks paying 7 Marks daily, paid for by Miss v. T. I remained in my profession until twenty-two years old; then I again had consumption and, since it did not improve, went to the institute for lung cure R. in the Black Forest where I stayed ten months and paid 3 Marks daily; Mrs. Hauptmann Q. and Miss v. T paid this, and then I returned to the boarding school and continued my profession until I was twenty-three. I then had stomach disease and returned to the deaconess house. There I stayed nine weeks. From there, I went to Mrs. Hauptmann's son, a pastor in D. (in Switzerland), where I stayed four months on account of the healthy air; since I was still sick, I helped the pastor's wife with the household work without needing to pay. I then returned to the boarding school where I took over the household duties since on doctor's orders I had to give up my other profession, because it was too stressful and I was rarely in the fresh air; but I had to soon leave as the illness flared up again and went to N. in the villa of the Baron v. T, which had been set up for the sick to recuperate, where I stayed five months. From there I went with the Baroness v. T. to M. (a Swiss city); we stayed there for two months, my position being to help the Baroness with her dressing, and received 70 Marks as a gift, this was not my profession, but I had to do it as her companion. Then we travelled to L. (a European capital) to the orphanage K., since the Baroness visited the poor children, as well as Sunday schools, kindergartens and young women's associations; after eight weeks we travelled from there to Y. and stayed there until I was twenty-six years old. I then went from Munich to Berlin to care for my

---

4 See on the founding of institutes for lung cure (*Lungenheil Anstalten*) in Switzerland: A. Käppeli, "Die Tuberkulose in der Schweiz, deren Verbreitung und bisherige Bekämpfung". *Der Schweizerischen statistischen Gesellschaft,* III-1, 1902, pp. 297–361, at p. 299.

sister. That was in November. I stayed with my sister until 15 January, then I worked in the hotel …. (First Class) as linen housekeeper where I was paid 30 Marks monthly. There I stayed until 1 June. I then stayed with my sister until 15 June during which time I met a man, who rented me a room in J. (a western suburb of Berlin); he paid me 8 Marks a day and I stayed there for 4 weeks until he suddenly disappeared. I then returned to Berlin and in the theatre met a Baron v. H., who only stayed in hotels, and I spent fourteen days drifting through life. I then associated with a Mr. v. G. with whom I travelled to F. (a large city on the Rhine) and returned on 4 September. I rented a room for which I had to pay 6.50 Marks daily, where I stayed until 30 September, when in the evening I was taken away by the vice police and bought to Froebel and that was the end of my former life.[5]

Anna Schlaff,

Allow me to request the Doctor's word of honour that this missive does not come into the public domain, since it may cause offence to illustrious persons. In this way, they will not discover the fate I have met.

I believe that by making all names and places unrecognisable, I have fulfilled Anna's wishes.

In order to evaluate this case, I would like to add the following to the letter: Anna had a rosy, blooming complexion, curvaceous body, and a friendly manner. When she was brought here by the police, she was suffering from general syphilis which was only cured with difficulty, since mercury poisoning set in. She volunteered to describe her life history when I asked other girls about their past. Whereas, at first impression, the untrained observer might conclude from her well-formed arms, imposing stature, well-developed bosom, and red cheeks that she was well-suited for work, this from my extensive observations only demonstrates how cautious one must be about the judgment "she may be able, but she is too lazy." Anna has one of those weak dispositions, who rarely succeed in work. She was

---

[5] The *Städtische Obdach* (the city shelter for the homeless) where Dr. Hammer worked as a *Hilfsarzt* (assistant physician) was located at Froebelstrasse 15, in Prenzlauerberg in Berlin. See for a brief history, Maritta Adam-Tkalec, "Obdachlose Frauen im Frauenasyl und Städtischen Obdach Berlin," *Berliner-Zeitung*, 15 February 2018. See also: Urte Verlohren, *Krankenhäuse in Groß-Berlin*, be-bra wissenschaft verlag, 2019, at p. 29.

not able to cope with religious duties since she became distressed, housework caused stomach pains, and work as a chambermaid made her lungs suffer. She tried to work here, washing and cleaning, resulting in a rash on the soft skin of her hands. When she engaged in prostitution, she became seriously ill after a short time. In her life story, the first thing that strikes one is the strong emphasis on money. In my opinion, this focus on money matters can be explained by the fact that while recording the description of each life I generally strongly emphasised the issue. There is no reason to doubt the truth of the content. In case of doubt, it is easy with the help of reference books (*Gothaer Hofkalender*,[6] Address Books[7]) to verify certain information. Scherl's address book collection Unter den Linden[8] was of great value in this respect; nevertheless, based on ten years' experience, I constantly checked the available handwriting of the girl. In this case, the handwriting revealed the following characteristics as plausible: trust, weakness, strong self-belief, a sense of cleanliness and tidiness, predominance of reason and emotional life over phantasy;[9] the handwriting samples, which ran to some one hundred lines, lacked the characteristics of falsehoods, although there are signs of sensuality. I accept the truth of the girl's narrative based on internal factors (none of which contradict it, and several of which

---

6   The *Gothaer Hofkalender* was a publication with details of the German nobility. See for details: <www.gotha-handbuecher.de/verlag.htm>.

7   August Scherl (1849–1921) published from 1896 the *Berliner Adreßbuch*, containing addresses of residents, businesses, and public authorities in Berlin. See archived copies at: digital.zlb.de/viewer/cms/141/. Scherl also published several regional German address books.

8   I could find no record of this collection. Unter den Linden is a principal boulevard in Berlin. A number of booksellers were based in Unter den Linden at the time, see: Wilhelm Junk, *International Adressbuch der Antiquar-Buchhändler*, Springer, 1906, at pp. 6, 10 and 18. The Berlin *Staatsbibliothek* at *Haus Unter den Linden*, which housed a collection of Scherl's Address Books, only opened in 1914.

9   The development of graphology as a diagnostic tool in medicine in German medical circles is examined by Igor J. Polianski, "Handschrift, Minderwertigkeit und Rasse: Die Schriftpathologie von ihren Anfängen bis zur Zeit des Nationalsozialismus / Handwriting, Inferiority and Race: Graphopathology from its beginnings to the time of National Socialism." *Medizinhistorisches Journal*, vol. 54, no. 2, 2019, pp. 108–44. *JSTOR*, <www.jstor.org/stable/45176657>.

support its veracity) and external (handwriting). If we try and answer the question how it happened that Anna took up prostitution, the following points are significant:

1. Anna evidently came from a family that was not wholly healthy. The mother died when she was five years old. A sister had to be cared for.
2. Anna herself is not completely healthy. She suffers repeatedly from catarrh in the lungs, as well as stomach illnesses and nervous indisposition – evidently her health is affected by the onset of consumption. It is an established fact that consumption stimulates people to engage in sexual intercourse. I also repeatedly observed that those suffering from consumption are strongly inclined to hedonism.
3. Anna lacked a maternal upbringing. After the death of her mother, she lived with an aunt until eight and then with a male relative. From then on, her education was irregular, with the result she had a submissive sense of respect for those of higher social rank.
4. This life spoilt the servant's daughter, whose obedient conduct, supported by a pretty appearance, won her the affection of wealthy circles. In addition, the orphaned child was pitied, so Anna was able to embark on European travel with a lady of high social rank.
5. Spoilt by a life of luxury, from early on exposed to all kinds of charitable deeds, she saw nothing discreditable in the fact of being paid. She accepted 200 Marks for the surrender of her virginity. She repeatedly let herself be supported by men.
6. She became so used to this life of luxury that she didn't take up the humble positions on offer. She wanted, as she told me, to be a nursemaid. However, after leaving she returned to prostitution and was placed under the control of the vice police.
7. It is neither hunger nor love, neither lack of bread nor excessive sensuality, but the passivity of her character, the inability to resist immediate temptations, the dazzling glitter of fashionable society, the veneration of those of higher social standing, these are the main reasons for her prostitution. This is the reason that here

I have called her Schlaff.[10] She looked with self-confidence at the list of all the nobles whom she frequented. But she is too weak to put the simple life of a nursemaid before the dazzling lustre of fornication. Used to the refined friendship of noble benefactors, she no longer wanted to obey ordinary bourgeois housewives, whose piercing commands and brusque reprimands seemed less bearable than the risk of once again catching the same disease she had already contracted. Her intermittent good intentions could not for long resist the weakness of her body and spirit.

I. On Prostitution and Prostitution Research

Prostitution is a diverse concept. According to von Düring at Kiel,[11] for 'us doctors' prostitution in the sense of a source of venereal diseases almost always coincides with the term 'extra-marital sex,' whereas for lawyers the prostitute is any person who without any other type of activity in exchange for payment offers themselves for sexual intercourse; they make a living from fornication.

I do not adopt any of these definitions, rather in this work I mean by female prostitutes those women who are handed over by the Berlin vice police for compulsory treatment. My purpose is to show ten life stories, the sort of girls who at this time are placed under the ordinances of the Berlin vice police. By this circumscription of the term prostitution, I am bound to reach different conclusions from those doctors for whom these words of von Düring apply, but also from those classes of society that denigrate

---

10   *Schlaff* means limp or flaccid.
11   Ernst von Düring (1858–1944) was Director of the Department of Dermatology at the University of Kiel from 1902–1906: C. Schirren and E.G. Jung, "Dermatology in Kiel: Fruitful Correlation of the Department of Dermatology with the Family Schirren," *Akte Dermatol*, vol. 32, no. 6, 2006, pp. 265–67, at p. 266. DOI 10.1055/s-2006-925303. In the period 1895 to 1905, von Düring published a number of articles on syphilis and its transmission, and a book *Klinische Vorlesungen über Syphilis*, published by Leopold Voss in 1895.

Gretchen in *Faust* as 'a whore.'[12] Gretchen's Valentine saw it proper while dying to curse his sister.[13] He summons the women to his place of death, for them to hear these words:

> My Margaret, see ! still young thou art,
> But not the least bit shrewd or smart,
> Thy business thus to slight :
> So this advice I beg thee heed–
> Now that thou art a – [whore] indeed,
> Why, be one then, outright !
> …
> The time I verily can discern
> When all the honest folk will turn
> From thee, thou jade ! and seek protection
> As from a corpse that breeds infection.
> Thy guilty heart shall then dismay thee,
> When they but look thee in the face :–
> Shalt not, in a golden chain array thee,
> Nor at the altar take thy place !
> Shalt not, in lace and ribbons flowing,
> Make merry when the dance is going !
> But in some corner, woe betide thee !
> Among the beggars and the cripples hide thee ;
> And so, though even God forgive,
> On earth a damned existence live ![14]

While until now it has been customary to treat prostitutes with contempt, I have avoided any demeaning statements about my patients.

Sine ira neque amore [without rage nor love.],[15] without partiality, I sought to research the life of over one hundred girls during their youth. I sought to gain the trust of my patients by means of conscientious medical treatment, so that the girls would willingly tell their life histories. I bound

12 Gretchen (Margaret) is a character in Part I of Goethe's *Faust* who drowns an illegitimate child she had from Faust.
13 Valentine is killed by Faust and dies in Gretchen's arms.
14 *Goethe's Faust*, edited by Elizabeth Craigmyle, Walter Scott, 1889, at pp. 163–64.
15 This is a rephrasing of "Tacitus' profession of impartiality at *Historiae* I, 1, 3 ('sed incoruptam fidem professis neque amore quisquam et sine odio dicendus est'): Marc Laureys, "'Sine Amore, Sine Odio Partium': Nicolaus Burgundius'

myself to each single girl to keep her name secret. At the same time, I explained to each girl the purpose of my research, scientifically to research the previous life of the prostituted girls, and that I did not seek any information against their will. "If you do not wish to tell me, your treatment is exactly the same as if you told me your life story. You are not required to answer my questions. On one matter I insist. If you give me information, please tell me the truth, for my part this will never result in any unpleasantness for you. Just as you can refuse to provide information about any questions, so you can refuse to answer any specific question. I prefer a refusal to provide information to false information. Would you like to make a statement?"

I put the questions to each girl that was willing to provide information, in a specific order on what I considered important points. I recorded the answers in shorthand. In order to obtain results that were least open to objection, according to the circumstances I primarily used the following means of verification.

For example, several times I interviewed a girl over several months. If exactly the same answers were given in the case of impromptu questions about specific points, then it was highly likely the statements were true. Another important means of corroboration was the previously mentioned Scherl's collection of address books, which is publicly available and free-of-charge. Another method I employed, was to seek information from a girl's former teacher. In addition, my own knowledge of the most important German cities and several German and foreign country districts served me well. On my travels, whenever I saw one of my previous patients, I engaged in conversation with her, wrote down her statements and placed the new document in the girl's file.

After my retirement from official positions, I received a whole range of helpfully retained documents of my former patients, which I could also use in part.

By these methods, I hope to make a worthwhile addition to the existing research which has mostly been restricted to statistics and surveys.

Historia Belgica (1629) and his Tacitean Quest for an Appropriate Past." *The Quest for an Appropriate Past in Literature, Art and Architecture*, edited by Karl A. E. Enenkel and Konrad A. Ottenheym, vol. 60, 2019, pp. 397–417, at p. 407. *JSTOR*, <www.jstor.org/stable/10.1163/j.ctvbqs5nk.22>.

2 Berta Wirt

(No. 4 in my files) was born in 185. in a small town in Thuringia. She was born in wedlock, in the Protestant faith. The father, a bricklayer, died in 189x; cause of death unknown. The mother died in 189x from a heart attack. From the age of 6 to 14, Berta attended the *Volksschule*.[1] She never repeated a class, she stayed two years in first class. From the age of 15 to 17, she did housework at home. There were two siblings. One sister is a house maid. Four sisters are dead. At 18, Berta worked as a maidservant in her hometown with the owner of a show booth (*Schaubuden*)[2] for an annual wage of 12 Talers.[3] The people toured annual markets. Berta was occupied at home with the family. She left: "I met someone there. A restaurateur from X. (a university town in Thuringia) took me with him." I took up as a waitress, "18 months in a position" until twenty-one. There I met my husband who married me when I was twenty-five. She lived sixteen years in a childless marriage until the death of her husband. In the university town, she married in 187. . In the same year, the married couple moved to a big city and

[1] "Children were enrolled in *Volkschulen* according to religious confessions and attendance was compulsory until age fourteen:" Ute Elisabeth Chamberlain, "Practical Reformers: Women School Owners in Imperial Germany." *History of Education Quarterly*, vol. 54, no. 4, 2014, pp. 465–85, at p. 469, n. 12. *JSTOR*, <www.jstor.org/stable/24482194>. See also: D. Skopp, "The Elementary School Teachers in "Revolt": Reform Proposals for Germany's Volksschulen in 1848 and 1849." *History of Education Quarterly*, vol. 2, no.3, 1982, pp. 341–61. DOI: 10.2307/367773; and Kenneth Barkin, "Social Control and the Volksschule in Vormärz Prussia." *Central European History*, vol. 16, no. 1, 1983, pp. 31–52. *JSTOR*, <www.jstor.org/stable/4545975>.
[2] See Stefan Nagel, *Schaubuden. Geschichte und Erscheinungsformen*. Münster 2000–2008. <www.schaubuden.de>.
[3] The Taler was replaced by the Mark from 1871–1873 but continued to be referred to in popular discourse. See: <www.bundesbank.de/resource/blob/607790/3fc8a459fd0205de5f902a904a7f69e1/mL/deutsche-taler-band-2-data.pdf>, at p. xxvi.

two years later to Berlin. In both cities, the couple ran a *Damenkneipe*[4] with "haughty service."[5] Her husband died in 189x from a heart condition. "I needed money and took up as barmaid."

1. Position: Berlin suburb.
2. Position: Berlin public house. She worked here for one and a half years. As waitress she had sexual intercourse with several men.

She received 5 pfennigs (Pf.) for each glass of beer.
A *Grätzer*[6] cost the client 25 Pf. and the waitress got 5 Pf.
Wine cost the client 500 Pf., the waitress got 50 Pf.
Champagne cost the client 1000 Pf., the waitress got 250 Pf.
"They had to be real idiots that came. We aroused them; took their money; threw them out."

In the same year, she was reported by a man. She was placed under police control.

In the same year, she had to attend a Berlin hospital on account of a miscarriage.

She planned to free herself from vice control by getting a position and then to reopen a *Damenkneipe*.

She gave the following information about her sexual circumstances:

---

4   "Damenkneipen (gemeint sind Lokale mit Damenbewirtung, jedoch keine Bordelle)...." ("Women's bars (meaning places with female hospitality, but yet not bordellos)..."; my trans.): Daniela Sandner, *Konstruierte Männlichkeit: Hygienische Reformliteratur, Prosatexte und Ego-Dokumente im Wilhelminismus und in der Weimarer Republik*, Roschbuch, 2019, at p. 291. DOI: doi.org/10.20378/irb-46531.

5   This is a translation of "mit schneidiger bedienung." Bedienung means service, as in a restaurant, and "schneidiger" is a word usually used in a military context to describe a person as "dashing." DWDS-Wörterbuch, an online german dictionary that provides examples of older usage of German terms, refers to the older meaning as: "knapp und abgehackt, gewollt markig und energisch, meist mit überheblicher Haltung verbunden" (brief, jerky, deliberately pithy, mostly associated with an arrogant attitude" (my trans.): <www.dwds.de/wb/schneidig>.

6   *Grätzer* is a type of beer named after the Polish town of Grätz where it was originally brewed: <https://pspd.org.pl/wp-content/uploads/2017/05/graetzer-brauwelt-1990.pdf>.

She was deflowered by her husband and experienced seven childbirths. The children are:

1. a boy born when the mother was 36 years old. She said the boy lived until 12 when he died of diphtheria;
2. a boy born when she was 38, who died of measles at 5 years old;
3. a girl born when the mother was 40. The girl was taken into the care of her grandmother in a university town in Thuringia and died aged 4 from diphtheria;
4. a girl, born when the mother was 44 years old, who died at 15 months from a septic tooth. "That happened during a relationship, which I still have with an unmarried goods merchant. However, he looks after me well, pays for my business and everything else;"
6 [sic]. a girl, still born in the sixth or seventh month when the mother was 46;
7. a breach baby girl,[7] when the mother was 48 (!) years old, "removed"[8] with her full consent.

She came to our hospital two years after she had been placed under the control of the Berlin vice police at the age of 43. She suffered from inflammation of the mouth and mucous patches on the buccal mucosa.[9] After twelve days she was cured and released. Her illness could be diagnosed as caused by a fully developed syphilis originating perhaps from twenty years ago. According to her statements, she had been a prostitute for already twenty years, and never been in treatment, except for one miscarriage.

7   The word used is "*gekippt*" meaning turned or tilted. I could find no example of usage of the word in this context in the period Dr. Hammer was writing. I have employed the term breach baby as this is occasionally a usage of *gekippt*.
8   The word used is "*ausgekratzt*". According to Duden, in a medical context, "*ausgekratzt*" means: "*Ausschabung, Abrasion, Kürettage*" (Dudenverlag, 1983, at p. 136). It refers to an operation, dilation and curettage, where part or all of the lining of the uterus is removed. This operation is also used as an abortion procedure, and this may have been the cause of the operation in light of potential health complications arising from Berta Wirt's age at the time.
9   A sign of secondary syphilis: Vijay Zawar, and Antonio Chuh. "Mucous patches and arthralgia." *Journal of the Royal Society of Medicine,* vol. 97, no. 2, 2004: pp. 79–80. DOI:10.1258/jrsm.97.2.79.

In approximately a ten-year period, she was admitted to hospital nineteen times. She did not make herself available and report regularly to the Königstrasse.[10] For that reason, she was sentenced to two years in the workhouse. There is strong reason to believe she scratched her sores to leave the workhouse. On our ward, she was a tireless worker. She was accomplished at housework, kept the rooms spotless, cleaned and scrubbed thoroughly and had a powerful physique. When I asked her why she did not make use of her industriousness to support herself on the outside, she replied:

"Really, where do you think I would find work outside? Here I work from desperation, just so I can endure it."

Her case gives rise to the following points of interest:

Berta could make a good living as housemaid. But she followed a man to a university town to work as a barmaid. The opinions of the Thuringian owner of the *Schaubuden* may have influenced her sense of morality. Annual fairground booths are in part travelling brothels. From waitress, she progressed to manageress of a *Damenkneipe*. Perhaps she was under the influence of her lover, who encouraged her into fornication and then married her. Her husband died of a heart attack induced by alcoholism. She had no savings, so she resumed work as a waitress. She takes pleasure in the exploitation of men. She took a particular pleasure in exploiting men by arousing them when she had no intention of satisfying them and then "throwing them out". In the city of intelligence,[11] there are many hundreds of bars, in which bad quality red wine (60 Pf. purchase price) is sold for 5 Marks, in which red wine is mixed in equal proportion with sparking mineral water and sold as champagne for 10 Marks, in which the waitresses' sole aim is to exploit the men. Many of the restaurants with *Damenkneipen* sustain a sordid existence in their cellars. Only a few upheld standards, since their waitresses allow contact that is strictly prohibited by the police. Because of the strict police control, it is not possible for the waitresses to service the clients in the separated rooms. Indeed, sitting on

10   The Berlin Polizeipräsidium (Police Headquarters) in Alexanderplatz was built in 1886–90 and located at the intersection of Dirkenstrasse and Alexanderstrasse. Königstrasse, since 1951 re-named Rathausstrasse, is an adjoining road and may have been used as an abbreviation by Dr. Hammer for the Police Headquarters.

11   In this period Berlin was referred to as 'Die Stadt der Intelligenz." See: Eduard Schmidt-Weissenfels, *Die Stadt der Intelligenz: Geschichten aus Berlin's Vor- und Nachmärz*, Seehagen, 1865.

the laps of the clients is not permitted. So, the exchange is limited to bawdy words and feeble attempts at lascivious fondling. The waitresses take care to drink along and finish off the *Grätzer*, a light beer in tulip glasses. According to the perceived stupidity of the client, they encourage him to order porter, a brown bitter beer, wine, mostly the most expensive red wine of bad quality, champagne. The girls are not paid a wage. They live off tips and these presents. A female innkeeper, who advertised for ladies with knowledge of languages, brazenly lied to the many girls who applied that through this work they would easily make three to four Marks a day. Her premises were only frequented by the finest gentlemen. But the girl must rent a room for 30 Marks, payable in advance. There were also girls who were incapable of earning one Mark a day and soon had to give up the position as they could not earn enough to live on. Of course, those who had been duped did not file a criminal complaint, and the manageress of the bar could again place her alluring advertisements. At 11 pm the *Damenkneipen* close. The waitresses go with a selected client to a café, where they let themselves be entertained. Occasionally, the client can afford the pleasure of spending the night with the girl, with the risk that he might be robbed or catch gonorrhoea as a souvenir of his "amusement." In most cases, however, the client is jettisoned. One night, I witnessed a scene off this kind in a busy street near to Alexanderplatz. A man of about thirty years old came out with two women from a *Damenkneipe*. The women wore striking, bright red hats and paid little attention to their companion. The man tried to get close to one of the women. But she ignored him, and when he did not keep his distance, there rang out from the delicate female mouth in a high treble voice the words: "Leave me in peace, you pig. Are you crazy, you brute!" The man obviously had nothing else in mind but to get away as quickly as possible, especially with the gaze of many passers-by directed at him.

II. The Berlin Vice Police and Their Consequences

Each female registered by the Berlin vice police as a public prostitute is handed a four-page printed document which is here reproduced word-for-word.

I. Police Regulations

to protect health, public order, and public decency, which came into force on 1 October 1902.

A female who, on account of engaging in prostitution, is placed under the control of the vice police and health authorities is subject to the following regulations:

1. She is required to undergo an examination by a doctor of her medical condition according to the following regulations:

The examination by a doctor takes place:
For prostitutes belonging to Class I twice a week,
For prostitutes belonging to Class II once a week,
For prostitutes belonging to Class III once every fortnight.

To Class I are assigned:

a) Prostitutes up to the end of their 24th year.

In addition, regardless of age:

b) Prostitutes who had been registered for not longer than one year.
c) Prostitutes with syphilis if three years have not elapsed since the first outbreak of syphilis.
d) Prostitutes who by their personality or their conduct (failure to comply with the police regulations, withdrawal from health controls etc.) or otherwise according to the judgment of the vice police, it is advisable to have their state of health diagnosed at frequent intervals.

To Class II are assigned:
Prostitutes between the age of 25 and 34, so long as they are not classified under Class I.

To Class III are assigned:

Prostitutes over 34 so long as they are not classified under Class I. The transfer of prostitutes from one class to another is decided by an order of the vice police.

2. She must punctually attend doctor's appointments and furthermore, as soon as she detects a venereal disease, she must report to the offices of the vice police. In the event this falls on a public holiday or festival day, she must present herself on the following weekday for examination by a doctor.
3. If diagnosed with a venereal or other infectious disease, she must present herself at the officially designated clinic until cured.

In the clinic, she must obey the orders of the physicians and supervisory authorities, as well as unconditionally comply with the house regulations.

4. She must wear simple and decent clothing. The wearing of men's clothing is forbidden.
5. On the streets and squares of the city she may not by her behaviour draw attention to herself. In particular, it is not permitted to stand or sit on streets, doorways, building entrances, or pavements, nor is it permitted to stroll up and down a limited area, nor in an offensive manner to flaunt herself, nor to allow herself to be seen in the company of a person whom she knows to be under the control of the vice police or to have been sentenced for procuring, or is known by her to be a pimp; nor is it permitted at a distance to wink or give any other sign to men to follow or speak to her.
6. It is forbidden to frequent the following streets and places except in cases of absolute necessity:

Lustgarten,
Tiergarten, including Königsplatzes,
Friedrichshain,
Humboldthain,
Viktoriapark,

Unter den Linden street,
Friedrichstraße from Oranienburgs Tor to Puttkamerstraße and Besselstraße,
Wilhelmstraße from Unter den Linden to Leipzigerstraße,
Potsdamerstraße,
Potsdamer Platz,
Königgrätzerstraße between Voß- and Köthenerstraße,
Königstraße,
Alexanderplatz and the adjoining open squares of Alexanderstraße,
Behrenstraße,
Leipzigerstraße,
Neue Wilhelmstraße,
Charlottenstraße und the intersecting streets between Charlotten- and Friedrichstraße,
Schadowstraße,
Neustädtische Kirchstraße, from Unter den Linden until Mittelstraße,
Kleine Kirchgasse,
Universitätsstraße, from Unter den Linden until Dorotheenstraße,
Kaisergalerie,
Opern-and Pariser Platz,
Platz am Zeughause,
Kastanienwäldchen.

In addition, it is forbidden to loiter in the vicinity of churches, schools, higher education institutes, imperial buildings, such as army barracks, to visit theatres, circuses, exhibitions, zoological and botanical gardens, museums, national train stations, both above and underground, unless holding a travel ticket, and in other places to be determined by police headquarters; in addition, it is prohibited to circulate in open carriages or bicycles on the prohibited places and streets.

7. In public bars, you may not draw attention to yourself by enticing men or forcing yourself on them. Smoking, making a loud noise and singing are prohibited, as well as entering into partitioned rooms in the bar.
8. You are prohibited from taking up any type of relationship with minors of male or female gender, and with pupils and school children at civil and military institutes.

9. You must pay attention that your presence in your dwelling or the vicinity does not give rise to any disturbance. If you fail to heed a warning, you are obliged to quit the premises within the period determined by the vice police.
10. You are obliged to permit or enable access day and night to your dwelling to the police for inspection of the premises and insofar as possible provide information about persons on the premises.
11. If you are found in a dwelling deemed by the police to be lodgings for prostitution, and if this activity has already given rise to complaints, the vice police can forbid you entry to these lodgings.
12. You are not allowed in any circumstances to show yourselves at the windows of your own or another person's premises.

During a visit from a man, the windows of your dwelling must be shut and covered with curtains in a manner to prevent any view into the dwelling. It is forbidden to place a lamp, a light, or any other sign at the window or in any other manner to seek to attract men from the window or the house entrance of your own or another premises.

13. You must on demand provide your correct address. You must personally report any change of address in the register of the vice police within three days, but at the latest by the next medical examination.
14. It is forbidden to loiter in the vicinity of churches, schools, higher education institutes, imperial and public buildings, in particular army barracks, as well as on the streets and squares access to which is prohibited under regulation no. 6 of these regulations, and to reside in the basement or ground floor of a house which faces the street. In addition, it is forbidden to reside in hotels, guest houses and boarding houses, or to enter such premises. Whenever it has been determined by the vice police that one of the housing situations listed under this regulation apply, and has given rise to offence, you are obliged to leave your dwelling within the period determined by the authorities.

15. Finally, it is prohibited for you to share your dwelling with another person, while you have a visit from a man, or to lodge your pimp in your dwelling.
16. It is forbidden to have an under-age person as a domestic servant.
17. You are obliged to keep secure your control book and legitimation card[12] delivered on dismissal[13] until handed over to the competent authority; it is prohibited to hand over either the control book or the legitimation card to a prostitute or any other unauthorised person.
18. While in the offices of the vice police, you must behave calmly and correctly and unquestioningly obey the orders of the supervising authorities and doctors.

Violation of these regulations is according to para. 361 no. 6 and para. 363 of the Penal Code of the German Reich[14] an offence punishable with up to six weeks imprisonment; furthermore, on completion of their sentence, the convicted person may be handed over to the state police authorities, who are authorised to transfer the person for a period of up to two years to a workhouse, a reformatory or educational institute, or to an asylum, or to employ her for socially useful work.

Berlin, 28 June 1902.
The Police Commissioner.

---

12 A legitimation card or *Legitimationskarte* was a document dating back to a Prussian Law of 1817 which could be issued to prove a person's identity; See: John Torpey, and Michel Charlot. "Le Contrôle des Passeports et la Liberté de Circulation. Le Cas de l'Allemagne au XIXᵉ. *Genèses*, no. 30, 1998, pp. 53–76, at pp. 59–60. *JSTOR*, <www.jstor.org/stable/26201788>.

13 Legitimation Cards were also used to authorise the exercise of trades and professions under a 1883 *Reichsgewerbeordnung*: (<www.deutscher-reichsanzeiger.de/rgbl/gewerbeordnung/>). The legitimation card could be retained by an employer and reasons for dismissal noted.

14 Adopted on 15 May 1871. See: Horst Schroder. "German Criminal Law and its Reform." *Duquesne Law Review*, vol. 4, no. 1, 1965, pp. 97–113, at p. 97.

II. Measures for the Prevention of Transmissible Venereal Diseases

1. It is prohibited to have intercourse with men whose urethra when pressed emits a mucus or pus-like discharge, or on whose penis enflamed or ulcerated parts are visible. Sexual intercourse with such men invariably results in infection.
2. After coitus, the sexual organs should be washed with water at room temperature and the vagina irrigated with lukewarm water by means of a rubber pipette or douche; for this purpose, a litre of water is to be used; the vaginal applicator is to be inserted about three inches into the vagina.

The same cleaning routine must be followed in the morning after getting up and in the evenings before going out.

3. In addition, in order to maintain the whole body clean frequent outdoor bathing in summer and at least weekly baths in winter are to be taken.

The greatest possible cleanliness of the whole body is an important protection against venereal diseases.

The official document comprises two parts. I. Police regulations issued to protect health, public order, and public decency. II. Measures for the prevention of transmissible venereal diseases.

The first part is signed without a name by "The Police Commissioner." The second part bears no signature.

Specifically, I would make the following comments:

A prostitute is not allowed to follow men, to stand on the street, to walk up and down in a restricted area, to sit. She is not allowed to attract the attention of other persons. She must for that reason take care to avoid any disturbance in her dwelling, and yet permit the officials from the vice police entry at any time of day or night. She is obliged at all times to follow police orders.

She must submit to hospital treatment if she has even the slightest suspicious bodily condition. This treatment is compulsory. Girls who do not submit are strapped down. Whether or not a girl is prepared to undergo a mercury treatment is not taken into consideration.

Whether the girl is burnt with the cautery knife, cut with a knife, treated with caustics, rubbed with mercury, is decided by the chief physician in the hospital.[15] Whether she is anaesthetised or not, whether she had to endure the pain while conscious, is not decided by the patients but by the doctors. The administrative inspector decides as judge whether a girl is to be placed in dark confinement, or should be punished by deprivation of food, or a fasting regime should be introduced to bring her under control. At the end of her period of suffering, the girl is rewarded with a bill of 2.50 Marks a day. Should it ever happen that, despite the regulations, a girl gets back on her feet or should ever come into an improved financial situation, then the enforcement officials make an appearance to collect the money for the compulsory treatment. All of this — to protect health, public order, and public decency. To protect health, public order, and public decency, Berlin's police officials go walking the streets seeking to identify which girls are engaged in prostitution. They are brought to police headquarters where they are examined by a woman, in case of illness presented to the doctor and brought to the hospital, given a warning, and if they are once again apprehended, placed under the control of the vice police.

Despite these controls, each adult male in Berlin will on average have 1.2 venereal diseases. In other words: out of 100 men on average 80 % will during their lifetime fall ill with gonorrhoea, 20 % with syphilis, and at least 20 % with soft chancres, scabies, and other rare infectious venereal diseases.

Some 150 specialist doctors for skin and urinary illnesses are based in Berlin. Each year a minimum of half-a-million Marks are spent in Berlin alone on physician fees for venereal diseases notwithstanding the "safeguarding" of health through the vice police regulations, which no woman under control can comply with fully if she does not want to starve. It almost

---

15 See Owsei Temkin, "Therapeutic Trends and the Treatment of Syphilis before 1900: In Memory of Max Neuburger." *Bulletin of the History of Medicine*, vol. 29, no. 4, 1955, pp. 309–16. *JSTOR*, <www.jstor.org/stable/44443951>.

seems as if the regulations serve to enable intervention at any moment against a prostitute; they express the spirit of the times, which sees in commercial prostitution an intrinsically immoral deed.[16] Prostitutes are used on one hand to satisfy male sexual pleasure but on the other subjected to strict discipline which extends over the most intimate aspects of their private life. (In official terminology: indecent glances at men; sufficient proof; a penal official).[17]

In the hospitals, the prostitutes were separated from the other patients, whereas on the male wards not even former convicts were separated. I am of the view that this measure is insufficiently justified if one disregards the viewpoint that public opinion must be considered. If a prostitute behaved among the other women in an insolent and disruptive manner, I would accept that segregation is justified. In other situations, I would consider it appropriate to house patients according to their illness and not on grounds of so-called decency. In cases where prostitutes were placed on a ward with other patients, I could at all times observe that they were thoroughly well-behaved.

16 Dr. Hammer uses the expression *"schlechte Handlung."* On this and other occasions, I have translated the word *schlecht* and its derivatives in such a context as immoral.
17 The meaning of this elliptical phrase is elucidated by the following: "eingeschrieben aber werden die Dirnen entweder auf ihren eigenen Antrag, oder wenn durch mehrfache Ertappung und Zeugnis mehrerer Polizeibeamter ihr Beruf unzweifelhaft nachgewiesen ist." ("prostitutes were either placed on the register at their own request, or their profession is unquestionably proven by means of multiple detection and evidence from several police officers;" my trans.): Kurt Wolzendorff, "Polizei und Prostitution. Eine Studie." *Zeitschrift Für Die Gesamte Staatswissenschaft / Journal of Institutional and Theoretical Economics*, vol. 67, no. 2, 1911, pp. 218–66, at p. 224. *JSTOR*, <www.jstor.org/stable/40743661>.

3 Christine Leichtfuss

(No. 9 in my files) furnished the following information.

Born 188., unmarried, Berlin, Protestant.

Her father, a butcher, died when she was ten. Her mother was a seamstress who married a potter. The potter died one year before Christine's birth. After one year's widowhood, Christine's mother gave birth to Christine. Christine did not know if the father paid alimony. She saw her father twice on the street but neither greeted each other, otherwise no contact. She attended the *Gemeindeschule*,[1] did not once repeat a class, spent one year and a half in first class, then was dispensed from classes for half a year because her mother needed her at home. From Easter to Winter, she sewed at home. Then she learnt to sew bodices at a firm in Berlin for four weeks. Afterwards, she was paid seven to eight Marks a week for piecework. This was insufficient, even though she lived at home, and she took a position as a barmaid. She always received food without lodgings, but nothing else; she changed position frequently. In NW. she was trained.

The client pays for:		Christine receives:
Grätzer —	25 Pf.	5 Pf.
Brausen[a] —	50 Pf.	10 Pf.
Porter —	100 Pf.	25 Pf.
Wine —	600 Pf.	100 Pf.
Champagne —	1000 to 1200 Pf.	200 Pf.
Champagne = ½ soda + ½ red wine.		

a *Brausen* are fizzy drinks with a variety of flavourings.

1 A local parish primary school. See: Peter Martin Roeder, "Gemeindeschule in Staatshand: Zur Schulpolitik des Preußischen Abgeordnetenhauses." *Zeitschrift für Pädagogik*, vol. 12, 1966, pp. 539–69; and B. Zymek, "Schulrecht und Schulentwicklung. Zum Verhältnis von Städten und Staat in der deutschen Schulgeschichte und heute." *Recht der Jugend und des Bildungswesens*, vol. 61, no. 4, 2013, pp. 484–504.

Wine: the client can order what he likes. He always gets the same bottle. Prices and labels vary.

Christine earns from 30 Pfennigs to 16 Marks daily. In one bar, she worked for eight months. The manageress was herself previously a barmaid.

She had her first period just before her confirmation. She lost her virginity just before reaching 16.

"I don't want to name the man. He owns a music shop. When I get out, I would again like to work as a barmaid in the street where he lives." They have fallen out at the moment because Christine was jealous. Did he not also have reason to be jealous? "That's my business." Otherwise, she had intercourse as a barmaid "with men whom she got to know there." She became pregnant from a farmer from Johannesburg, who now has moved to Canada. "I was meant to follow," but her legal guardian,[2] a lawyer, did not permit it, he banned Christine as a barmaid from going.

(Evidently, it concerned a client of the bar who in every respect made a fool of her).

Illnesses: as a child healthy.

At fifteen, first treatment for syphilis.

At sixteen, second treatment for syphilis. ("'Mother said, I should go to the hospital.")

At seventeen: Christine had a still birth in the seventh month. Eight days after the birth, Christine left the maternity hospital; she lived with her mother and in the evenings worked as a barmaid in the north of Berlin. She changed position and went to work in a *Damenkneipe* just opposite, her clientele followed. Her former innkeeper, whom she had taken the clients from, reported her for having gone to a dance hall with clients. As a result, she was brought by the police to the Fröbel hospital.

Christine is of medium height, strong, with a healthy appearance; she has smoked since she was thirteen. "I prefer to not to eat anything, but I must smoke. Every day I smoke between 50 and 60 cigarettes, when I am having a good time."

---

2   The appointment of a legal guardian to a minor whose father had died was regulated by paragraph 1698 of the Civil Code of 18 August 1896, which came into force on 1 January 1900.

Her handwriting is ornate, with sudden points of pressure, heavily marked (sensuality, craving for admiration).

She plans to work again as a barmaid and live near to her beloved, the musical instrument dealer. On our ward she masturbates regularly. The girls who do not (3 to 4 out of 60 girls) are mocked. She also has a girlfriend outside.

When she was released, she entered a welfare institute; for four days she was employed, but then left. She went to her mother. There she got a beating. The mother wrote to the female pastor in charge of the institute. When Christine discovered she was to be sent back, she left her mother's. Now she lives off prostitution. On the street she earns a minimum of 10, at most 25 Marks a day. She has intercourse every day, "depending on what sort of man it is," with from one to three men. If she has money left, she does not go out in the evening. Otherwise, she frequents the dance halls. She pays 6 Marks a day for board and lodgings, at the beginning of Elsasser Straße,[3] with two stairways, and an entrance hall. The landlady had herself previously been under vice police control. Once she waited for her unspoken love, the music shop owner, without speaking to him.

After one and a half weeks Christine was arrested on the street and, after being taken to the police headquarters, handed over to the Fröbel hospital.

She has four deceased siblings, who all died in early youth; two living siblings, one is 24 years old and is under police control for about four years (stepsister from the same mother, also treated at the Fröbel hospital). The younger 22-year-old sister was a worker in a light bulb factory and then married a factory worker.

"My mother knows what I am like. I am a little bit reckless, but otherwise not bad. Or at least so my mother tells me. I will continue as a barmaid and love my position. No matter how long you lock me up for. I will never be a housemaid."

---

3   A street in Berlin near the Oranienburger Tor, renowned for its variety halls. In 1951 it was merged with Lothringer Strasse and in 1994 renamed Torstrasse. See: <www.gerhildkomander.de/strassen/197-berliner-strassen-torstrasse.html>.

In assessment of this case, I would note the following: Christine displays a serious innate hindrance[4] which has not been significantly lessened by her upbringing. The mother gave birth one year after the death of her husband. One of her siblings born from the same mother is under police control. A second sister gave birth twice out of wedlock from two men.

The moral views at her parental home were so lax that the daughter could not be sheltered from sexual intercourse. Even if the mother had supported herself, even had she nurtured a child's success until the age of 14,[5] even so two daughters lacked sufficient patience to maintain a proper post. A middle daughter gave birth out of wedlock, but still remained a factory worker. She also became a married woman, while the other two girls became prostitutes.

The beatings by the mother, which were mostly in these circles inflicted with a carpet beater, failed because the mother's past life was not irreproachable. In my experience, it is scarcely possible to convince children, whose parents lead a licentious life, that in engaging in a life of unchastity they do something wrong. This holds true already in the case of the father's adultery, but even more from the unchastity of the mother and the father. If a good example is lacking, the cane is of little use. Christine, by nature a talented child, lacked any paternal upbringing. The father did not look after the mother and child, and thus gave an even worse example than the mother. The guardian did not properly devote himself to his charge. The welfare institute failed utterly.

---

4   The German word *"Belastung,"* translated here as hindrance, refers in a medical context to a "hereditary taint (or tendency):" *Langenscheidt's Encyclopaedic Dictionary of the English and German Languages*, Part II German-English, vol. 1, edited by Otto Springer, Langenscheidt, 1983, at p. 241.
5   The age at which enrolment at the local *Volksschule* ended.

III. Training of Young Prostitutes

Until the age of 18, if a young woman is brought to Court on account of prostitution, she is sent for welfare training.[6]

Those who support welfare training argue that prisons are not places of improvement, but instead where new groups are constantly led astray into a bad way of life. If we ask ourselves which prison conditions facilitate the downfall of young inmates, we must principally blame the communal living of a large number of people with the same mindset. The regulated life, the strict discipline, the structured work, the simple diet, can hardly be treated as responsible for aggravating the situation. Rather, the principal cause of this aggravation in the reformatories, just as in the prisons, is the presence of mutual seduction; even in the absence of older prostitutes, the communal living of many girls, often more than one hundred, previously engaged in prostitution, leads to their mutual induction into the darkest areas of sexual deviance. Until now, I have never seen any success resulting from the institutional training of prostitutes. On the contrary, the following rule can be deduced from my observation of the girls in welfare training: the longer a girl stays, the more certain it is she will be determined after her release to resume a life of prostitution. The longer the detention lasts, the more pronounced are the dysfunctions caused by chastity. Amongst the many dozens of girls entrusted to welfare training, I could not find one who had been noticeably improved. Of the twenty-five pupils in the reformatories, twenty-two were engaged in same sex amorous activity, or were strongly suspected of being lesbian. Of the three remaining girls, another was identified as lesbian within a month.

Of some sixty girls, fifty-six engaged in masturbation. Anyone who did not was mocked. Not one of the girls in welfare training known to me had learnt a trade. Housework and simple crafts were the only skills the girls had acquired.

---

6   The transfer of minors into reformatories was regulated by the Prussian Law on the Welfare Training of Minors (*Gesetz über die Fürsorgeerziehung Minderjähriger*) of 2 July 1900.

The typical training methods employed to date are:

1. Termination of any contact with the outside world or men. Even the work of the doctor and the pastor is in part handed over to females. There are no excursions, nor any visits to attractions. Relatives only occasionally are allowed to visit.
2. The whole day is strictly divided; with detailed instructions for each hour; discipline at mealtimes, work, walks in the garden.
3. Exposure to religion. One or two hours of basic instruction each week.
4. Punishment by deprivation of food, conversation; further measures include solitary confinement in dark cells with bunk beds and minimal clothing. As a last resort, through extension of the period of detention for training.

Although I got to know dozens of girls who had been in welfare training, I could not identify one whose character was improved by this manner of institutional training. I also could not find any girl who considered this institutional training to be of benefit.

Furthermore, I did not observe that the girls had learnt a sustainable trade other than housework and needlework. While giving full recognition to the painstaking and often thankless work of the pressurised teachers in reformatories, I consider that in light of the minimal success achieved so far that it is advisable that training and education be combined in these institutions to a greater extent than at present, if indeed it is planned to persevere in the building of such institutions. The girls are in most cases required to spend two years as the minimum period of incarceration. In two years, certain trades can be taught and learnt. Perhaps, at some point, it will be attempted to teach the girls a sustainable trade in the same manner as male trades, e.g., book binding, book printing, tailoring. In this case, it is important that the girls learn a trade proficiently and practice as long as necessary so as to be able to support themselves with the acquired trade.

In this manner, training and education go hand in hand. Without doubt it would provide the girls with greater motivation. Particularly hardworking girls could have the opportunity to earn treats, trinkets, or jewellery items. Furthermore, girls who performed additional tasks could, in recognition of their extra work, be released early. Proficient girls could supervise the inexperienced. The reason for poor performance should be identified and addressed as necessary, in the case of lack of aptitude through the provision of caring and individual instruction, in case of physical weakness by allocating light work, in case of laziness or ill-will by appropriate punishment. Because I consider a healthy diet a key requirement, I am of the opinion that a starvation diet and solitary confinement should preferably be replaced by beatings.[7] Beatings to be effective should not be too harsh, nor too soft, the latter to avoid arousing perverse feelings. Therefore, each teacher must be given a code of conduct setting out how far she is entitled to go. Perhaps in this way classes could be established, so that a girl through her good conduct could advance. In the higher classes, the cane could be done away with. In the case of repeated bad behaviour, a return to the lower classes would have to be possible. I consider that whippings that cause blood to flow, as earlier practiced in prisons, are not appropriate in reformatories. A relaxed atmosphere should prevail during work and leisure time. The cane must be more feared than used.

If this approach were adopted, life in the institutions would be more bearable. Many girls would discover the blessings of a proper position and learn to treasure it. Lasting success is, however, difficult to achieve, since the sexual drive is powerful even in the case of strenuous work accompanied by a healthy diet. So long as proceedings for prostitution offences involve summoning one half of those involved (the male party) as respectable witnesses for the prosecution, while the other half (the female party) must sit in the dock as poor sinners, it is difficult to convince a girl, who sees herself as created for intercourse with multiple men and the intoxicating life of fornication, that injustice has not been committed. Neither painful gynaecological diseases, nor the sight over several weeks of the suffering of syphilitic companions in misfortune, frighten to any significant degree the girls inclined to prostitution into abandoning their plans. Religious

---

7   For a description of Dr. Hammer's advocacy of corporal punishment and his attempt to determine scientifically the most effective level of punishment, see: Jazbinsek, *supra,* at pp. 46–48.

and moral precepts have proven to have just as little effect on these girls as on the men with whom they associate.

If one were to extend the recently expanded welfare training from the institutions into the family, then the educator must be given full legal authority. Where is one to find families willing to sacrifice themselves, to devote themselves to this selfless and thankless task? The choice would not be extensive, especially since a badly brought-up child is more likely to lead his comrades into wrongdoing, than a well-brought up one is to lead them into goodness, a thought which our Father conveyed in his teaching on original sin. But even well-suited families often fail in this area, since it is absolutely impossible to achieve durable success in the case of many of these girls. Every effort, every selfless act, every good intention, every indulgence, and every act of discipline, fail if the mind has reached a certain level of deviation from the mean.

4 Dorothea Schwächlich[1]

(No. 106 in my files)

My research into prostitution took me in various directions. One Sunday during visiting hours, the father of one of my welfare patients visited and asked for information about his seriously sick daughter. He gave the impression of a conscientious civil servant and voiced his distress in poignant terms. I listened and provided him with information about his daughter. A short time later, he again made contact. A religious association had proposed his daughter for welfare training, and he asked for my advice. I strongly advised against giving his consent to welfare training, and at the same time sought his permission personally to find out more about his circumstances. He willingly gave me his permission. A short time later, I travelled to Silesia.[2] There, I received a letter with the following content:

Berlin, (Date)
Dear Doctor,

I herewith urgently request you not to visit the workplaces of my older children, since this could cause them difficulties, and it would be very painful for them to discuss in the presence of others these distressing family circumstances, but my house is at all times open to you.

---

1   *Schwächlich* means frail or feeble.
2   From 1763 to 1918, the greater part of Silesia (Schlesien), a geographical area bordering the river Oder, was part of Prussia. See, on the close connections between Berlin and Silesia: Roswitha Schieb, *Jeder Zweite Berliner: Schleschiche Spuren auf der Spree,* Potsdam, 2012.

Yours sincerely,
....
... Street, ... III. l[3]

I promptly replied to the letter, as is my custom, and carefully filed the letter, the striking regularity of whose traits made a good impression. Half a year later, long after Dorothea had left the hospital and was staying in a welfare foundation, I travelled for ten Pfennigs to the furthest northern part of Berlin. It was early evening. The manual workers in their hundreds left the factories for home. The multitude of children of the impoverished local population played on the streets. Goods merchants offered their wares, besieged by women with sallow and furrowed faces. Other women collected their husbands from the workplace, so that the wages would not be squandered. In between, one could hear the shrill bells of the electric trains, the clanking wheels of the trucks, the heated voices of the street traders. Women with tired, sallow faces crept out of the stores and workplaces heading towards their tenements. In one of these tenements lived thirty-three families. A restaurant was operated in the front house, a carpentry workshop in the courtyard.

The cobbled courtyard was enclosed by a side wing on the left and right. In the entrance near the door, the mute porter supplied the requested information. I climbed the stairs, on each floor lived three families, one on the right, one on the left, and one straight ahead.

After I had climbed three flights of stairs, I discovered the Schwächlichs had moved. I went to their new dwelling. When I rang, a woman opened and immediately closed the door again. I rang again, and was, as I had envisioned, warmly greeted, and led into the parlour. The parlour was kept impeccably clean and tidy, unsparingly furnished. There were also ornaments. I asked where the daughter was at present. In ... foundation. The woman willingly replied to my further questions. The cost of her education was not charged to her. Her father had visited. A gentleman was present and had inspected everything. Until now no bill has been received. The

---

3 This is a reference to the number of the *Stadtteile,* of which there were 12 in Berlin, where the street address was located. No. III. was Friedrichs-Werder. See: *Die Berliner Volks-Zählung vom 3 December 1861,* Julius Sittenfeld, 1863, at p. 71.

fine furniture had been provided by her oldest daughter. She was soon to be married. Dorothea, who is now in the foundation, is 18 years old. She has an older brother. He is 21 years old, is bookkeeper and earns 90 Marks a month. A 19-year-old sister is sales assistant in a wallpaper business and earns 60 marks monthly. Another sister is apprentice in a porcelain shop.

A 13-year-old brother is in *Volksschule*, has never repeated a class. In fact, he won a prize.

The mother suffers from nervous illness and Basedow's disease,[4] which sometimes confines her to bed.

The father now has 23 years' service, a demanding position, but is completely healthy.

Dorothea was from a young age scrofulous,[5] as a child she required protective glasses, was hysterical, vexed by every trifle, stubborn, and is now in a foundation. "That I had to have such a child."

When I asked her if she didn't always forgive men who "did such things," the mother replied: "a young man can do that, as he wishes." If she permits men to do such things, she must then also allow girls to indulge themselves! "But for money! That I should have such a child! People would point their finger at me if they knew!"

I comforted the mother, pointing out public opinion's lack of compassion. My dear lady, now you have learnt that it is not only the parents who deserve credit when the children turn out well, and that despite every effort a child can go astray.

Then she further explained that Dorothea had never repeated class at school, she spent two years in first class in the *Gemeindeschule*.

After leaving school she should have remained at home. "No," she said "that's impossible. I must be of use, learn something." She did not want to be placed in a position. She found positions herself. In Berlin C. she completed a year's apprenticeship as shop assistant. She earned 10

---

4 "**Thyrotoxicosis or Basedow's disease**: A disease due to overactivity of the thyroid gland. It produces a goitre, accelerated metabolism in the body, loss of weight, fast heart action, mental irritability and sometimes exophthalmos." A. S. Playfair, *The Essential Medical Dictionary*, Chancellor Press, 1990, at p. 233.
5 "Scrofula. An old name for tuberculosis involving the lymph glands of the neck." Ibid, at p. 207.

Marks monthly. She always handed me the 10 Marks. So far, she was well-behaved. She kept one Mark for pocket money. I bought candy from time to time, the children had as much as they needed. She always got food and clothing. She didn't lack for anything. There was always enough to eat. But then she didn't want to continue there any longer. Her boss was opposed to her leaving. She stopped going, she lied to me for two months. She travelled there, purchased travel tickets. Everything's fine, mother, I am getting 40 Marks a month. Three days later she went to … Street (in the Tiergarten district)[6] and borrowed 50 Marks. Father and I were dead. She needed the money for coffins. The money would be reimbursed to her by the authorities. The people asked me whether the facts were true, and immediately denounced her for swindling. At nine o'clock, as always, she returned "from the business!" She no longer denied it, said that she held a position as cleaning lady with an artist. The complaints could no longer be withdrawn. As a result, she received a caution from the Court. Then I kept her at home until April (the year in which she was 16).

If only she would stop causing me trouble. Then, until July she was assistant to the housekeeper with Mrs. X. in a suburb. In July she left. She had not been obedient. I was ill and had to travel to Z. and took three children with me. The day before my departure, I received a pneumatic postcard:[7] Dorothea departed, destination unknown. It was a teacher's family. She received 15 Marks monthly and everything was free of charge, she was then 16 years old. She stayed away for eight days. She came back completely filthy, as if she had slept on the heath. I kept her at home. Then her former boss took her back. He said she was hard-working and orderly. After four weeks she suddenly stayed away. At first, she didn't take any money and disappeared for three months. She often telephoned her brother: I am well; everything's going fine; then, he should come to a restaurant. Then we collected her from Tieckstrasse[8] (… obviously, after she was apprehended by the police). Her hair was infested with louse. She said she had been an assistant to an actress. She lied. It frightened me. Then she

6   A district in central Berlin.
7   The pneumatic *Stadtrohrpost* or pneumatic postal system in Berlin was commissioned in 1865: see, <https://pneumatic.tube/mail-berlin-germany>.
8   A street in the centre of Berlin.

was kept at home. A gentleman came from the welfare authorities. I didn't hand her over. A female pastor ... came. She took her on as housekeeper. For 10 Marks a month she had to look after the household of a merchant. After four months, she stayed away due to the travelling as far as the south east [of Berlin]. She had to be there on time. She never went back, instead she was taken by the police to the Fröbel hospital on account of abdominal pains and from there transferred to a welfare foundation.

"Her father?" He won't see her anymore. A female pastor, who wanted to bring her into the foundation, said: then at least she will be taken off the streets for a while. In her most recent letter, she wrote: Doctor Hammer is travelling. If you write to him, please pass on my greetings. Send me belongings. A gentleman came: they were taken away.

The female pastor ... told me, when I asked her to be allowed to keep the girl, that it was impossible. Once she had been engaged in prostitution, the parents have no more authority. "But I have ..." I told her. I urged her to allow Dorothea to stay at home. The female pastor said: she leaves and straightaway she is ruined (probably a misunderstanding of Mrs. Schwächlich).

I again advised her to keep her daughter, since there was no hope of improvement through the institution, and proposed she arrange a consultation with the head of the foundation. I also did not hide from her that by innate brain abnormalities, even in the case of attentive individual education, I observed failures more often than successes.

In the kitchen, I met a younger brother of Dorothea, a 13-year-old pupil in the *Gemeindeschule* who was struggling to name a field plant in accordance with Linnaeus.[9] I helped the talented and charming child, and within a few minutes he had found the class, rank, and name.[10]

Then I took my leave of the civil service family. As I set foot on the street, it was already dark. Adolescents of both sexes were being swung around rapidly on carousels, while street organs strove to accentuate their tunes in shrill confusion. The city nightlife had started. From the thousands of bars selling alcohol, came the raucous sound of men's voices. On

9   Carl Linnaeus (1707–1778) was a Swedish botanist who developed a system for classifying plants.
10 See on Linnaeus' classification: Magnus Lidén, "The Legacy of Linnaeus." *BGjournal*, vol. 4, no. 1, 2007, pp. 4–7, at p. 5. *JSTOR*, <www.jstor.org/stable/24810402>.

the brightly lit Friedrichstrasse,[11] walked well-dressed men, women wafted by. Six times in a short time my name was called by former patients, never in an unfriendly manner. Past the Hallesches Tor,[12] the city slept. Only here and there a girl crept past me or targeted the bachelor lodgings of a single man …

Evaluation: Dorothea has without suffering from destitution embarked on a life of fornication, in spite of a good and conscientious education, in spite of a satisfactory position. None of her siblings have ended up like her. Both parents are thoroughly dutiful and hard-working. Dorothea behaved, so long as I could observe her, in a docile manner and receptive to remorse. When I turned the conversation to her father, she wept bitterly. Her conduct was thoroughly tidy and hard-working. As the main reason for her change to a debauched lifestyle, I saw as a weakness towards external influences. As her body was afflicted in childhood from serious illnesses, as during her puberty according to her mother she was "hysterical", so when afflicted with venereal diseases she could only muster limited powers of resistance (she was bedridden for several weeks because of jaundice), so she was also feeble in resisting carnal temptations, whose priestesses, according to the opinion of "reputable" women, lead a life full of bliss and pleasure. Sweet idleness seems wonderful to her. Lacking sufficient wisdom, she hoped in her folly that by means of false pretences she could pay back the money. Obviously the 50 Marks she acquired in the Tiergarten district was only investment capital that would be invested in fine clothing and night cafés and would bear a handsome return. The calculation was intrinsically false. Men who pay willingly are rare, much more so than women who want to be paid, and the novice also earns little as a prostitute, often not enough for the necessities of life, and even when one or another man pays, then is he often diseased, and with a few Marks or Groschen seeks to appease his conscience. Thus, Dorothea quickly ended up destitute. Reimbursement was out of the question. The few paying clients had sufficed to make her ill.

---

11 A street in central Berlin.
12 Site of a former gate in 18–19th-Century Berlin – now the site of an underground station in Kreuzberg.

IV. On the Sexual Question

The sexual question cannot be resolved through a one-sided approach. Here the issue is rather treated in light of the necessary appraisal of the ethical, legal, health and economic factors in order to determine the desired goals and appropriate means. In this brief text, I will only raise certain issues, without making any claim for completeness.

1. From an ethical perspective, it is important to question whether sexual intercourse is also ethically permissible or advisable for purposes other than reproduction. If it is ethically permissible to obtain sexual release as an end in itself, perhaps through bringing about the effective release of nervous tension, then advice on contraceptive methods is ethically allowed. If it is ethically permissible for males of questionable character to satisfy their sexual drive[13] outside of marriage, then there must also be an ethically permissible form of intercourse outside of marriage for women. In other words: if men have intercourse with prostitutes, without thereby falling into immorality, then women cannot be considered immoral because they engage in intercourse with men. It is conceivable that chastity is required of married women before marriage, but not for men. If so, prostitutes are not suitable for marriage, but are not to be treated as immoral. It is to be treated as a form of division of labour.

2. The relevant laws would be evaluated as to whether the existing provisions are absolutely necessary for the harmonious coexistence of members of society, or whether without any significant harm a series of measures could be abolished.

3. As regards health issues, the following question arises: Is sexual abstinence healthy or not? I have set out my position at length in "Die

---

[13] Dr. Hammer uses the word "*Liebestrieb*." Freud was later to use the term to designate the eros drive in contrast to "*Todestrieb*" or the death drive in *Beyond the Pleasure Principle* (1920).

gesundheitlichen Gefahren der geschlechtlichen Enthaltsamkeit"[14] (published in 1904 by Malende, Leipzig, available at 80 Pfennigs)[15] and note here only the following:

Sexual abstinence in the age of sexually maturity presents risks for both sexes. These risks are in part avoidable through other means than sexual intercourse, but only partially. From a purely health perspective, abstinence is not to be recommended either for men or women if they have the opportunity to release their psychic and physical desires without detriment. However, the question cannot be resolved simply on health grounds. As regards the risk of syphilis, I consider the testing of prostitutes in itself as ineffective. The girls released from the hospitals are as a rule not completely free of risk. Uncontrolled sexual intercourse of many girls with many men is the primary means of transmission of venereal diseases.

If one was willing to acknowledge prostitution, then one could significantly reduce the possibilities of infection by establishing brothels with general practitioners, whereby each client and each girl would be examined and healthy men associated with healthy girls, and diseased men with girls who suffered from the same disease. At the same time, every preventive measure should be recommended. Otherwise, I consider brothels to be dangerous, as they only offer the appearance of protection, but not effective protection. Nearly all the favourable statistics presented in respect of brothels are based on circumstances in which men and women are placed under control (military); over the years, I have not seen a single man, who has regularly satisfied his sexual urges in a brothel, who has not

---

14 "The health risks of sexual abstinence" (my trans.).
15 Dr Hammer's publication was twenty pages in length with two illustrations, *Gesamtverzeichnis des deutschsprachigen Schrifttums (GV)*, edited by Hilmar Schmuck and Willi Gorzny, K.G. Saur, 1982, at p. 251. Dr. Hammer's publication is commented on at p. 397 of Volume 1 of *Geschlecht und Gesellschaft*, edited by Karl Vanselow, Verlag der Schönheit, 1905, and at p. 193 of *Studies in the Psychology of Sex*, vol. 6, by Havelock Ellis, Outlook, 2018. Dr. Hammer published an article "Geschlechtliche Enthaltsamkeit und Gesundheitsstörung" ("sexual abstinence and health disorders," my trans.) in *Monatsschrift für Harnkrankheiten und sexuelle Hygiene*, vol. 5, 1904, pp. 214–17.

been infected. Furthermore, for my part, it is utterly incomprehensible why adherents of control assist in the ruination of the girls, in that they exclude them from all the benefits of labour insurance, but still require them to bear the costs of the compulsory treatment. Currently I consider that even in Berlin, where there are no brothels recognized by the police, that sexual intercourse with prostitutes, that is with girls who over a short period of time frequently prostitute themselves with men, is a near certain path to gonorrhoea and other venereal diseases. I am of the opinion that a significant increase in venereal diseases through the possible abolition of compulsory examinations is unlikely.

4. Finally, as concerns the economic aspects of the question, I consider the following points to be worth mentioning.

Firstly, the question of whether marriage as currently constituted is the only secure foundation for a thriving development of our people, is an important one. If this question is answered in the affirmative, then the further one is to be debated, whether alongside marriage another form of sexual intercourse is to be recognized. If so, also this question raises another difficulty, what form of extra-marital sexual intercourse should be recognised and protected, whether during the lengthy period of bonding of a couple (concubinage) or the frenzied sexual intercourse of multiple men with multiple women (promiscuity) or finally the mixing of a few women with many men (prostitution). If, however, agreement is reached on the second question, so that only monogamy is acknowledged, then the question arises whether the earthly punishment of the deviant behaviour is to be recommended, or whether reference to the Last Judgment as the highest and infallible authority, as well as the moral influence on mankind, suffices.

If ongoing research should demonstrate that a nation's downfall, growth and aggressive expansion coincides chronologically with so-called dissolute sexual mixing (extra-marital intercourse, prostitution, pederasty, lesbianism, sadomasochism), it still leaves the causal connection unclear. If we mean by a nation's downfall, loss of a people's independence, then the following reflection is possible: when the struggle for existence also reigns among national groupings, and when the rule of conservation of energy also applies to humans, then every nation is doomed to destruction.[16] It follows there would be for every nation a state of youth, a state of maturity and a state of old age. If we then postulate a certain sum of energy in a nation, then a diverse division of this sum of energy is possible. A nation can be preeminent physically, it can also pursue excellence in the development of intellectual capacities. According to the law of conservation of energy, the sum of energy cannot be increased. Thus, an increase in intellectual capacities must lead to a decline in other forces, perhaps muscular strength. When can a young nation subjugate an old one? Evidently, in every case when it disposes of greater physical capacities of resistance and at the same time is capable of appropriating the intellectual achievements of the older nation. Uneducated nations endowed with brute physical strength are not guaranteed superiority over educated races if they do not succeed in taking advantage of the intellectual achievements of the older nation. In battles between two nations of equal size, the younger one will vanquish through imitation (reproduction) the moment it exploits the inventions of the older nation. Inventions require higher intellectual capacities than imitation. The imitating nation will conquer despite inferior intellectual capacities because it disposes of superior physical powers of resistance and at the same time adopts the achievements of the intellectually superior nation. These phenomena, which many consider to be the origins of the downfall, e.g., the flourishing of the women's rights movement,[17] the increase in confirmed bachelors, the rise in entitlements, could be no more than

---

16   The law on the conversation of energy had been the subject of a mathematical treatise by Ernst Mach (1838–1916), *History and Root of the Principle of the Conservation of Energy* originally published in 1872. See also: G. Sarton, et al. "The Discovery of the Law of Conservation of Energy." *Isis*, vol. 13, no. 1, 1929, pp. 18–44. *JSTOR*, <www.jstor.org/stable/224595>. Theories about the causes of the decline of civilisation can be traced back to Giambattista Vico (1668–1774): see Patrick H. Hutton, "Vico and the End of History." *Historical Reflections / Réflexions Historiques*, vol. 22, no. 3, 1996, pp. 537–558. *JSTOR*, <www.jstor.org/stable/41299074>. More generally, see: Francis Neilson, "The Decline of Civilizations." *The American Journal of Economics and Sociology*, vol. 4, no. 4, 1945, pp. 479–497. *JSTOR*, <www.jstor.org/stable/3484150>.

17   For the criticism directed at Dr. Hammer by the women's movement in Germany, and in particular by Ella Mensch (1859–1935), see Jazbinsek, *supra*, at pp. 36–37.

the manifestations of old age. While black dye on white hair may bestow a younger appearance, it never results in a more highly developed old age. Struggling against the signs of the onset of decay will not hold back the collapse if the perspective just set out is correct. A doctor's task is to alleviate the death of an old man, but not to advise him to behave like a man of strength. When a nation has reached the end of its life cycle, then it has no sense to advise marriage and begetting many children.

It is not proven that this opinion is correct. Nonetheless it is possible. In any event the proposals for reform are dependent on the stance that the adviser adopts to the question: has our nation arrived at its old age or is our nation still in its vigorous prime?

5 Elsa Streng[1]

(No. 96 in my files)

23 years old, born in wedlock, of Catholic confession, born in a large west German city.

Father: Supervisor in a west German mine, deceased.

Mother is alive and was healthy when Elsa had news of her five months ago.

She hadn't written home in the last five months, "since I am not allowed to return home at the moment. When you have sunk so low, then I can't return home. I know that if you come from a strict family."

From the age of 6 to 14 she attended the *Elementarschule*[2] in a small, west German locality. She never repeated a year, was four years in first class (obviously in a two-class *Gemeindeschule*). At the end of her school age, she received a year's private education. Then she spent two years in a convent where she participated in various religious practices. The convent in question is renowned. From there, Elsa attended for a year and a half the *Selekta*[3] in a small town of her region. Then she stayed at home for half a year and helped her father who, after his accident in the mine, was engaged in the preparation of written documents.

She then passed the female teacher's exam in the Rhine province. She was not, however, appointed "due to oversupply." The town where she underwent her seminary training had to let her go. At the end of the half-year, the director had suggested that she had received a male

---

1 *Streng* means strict or severe.
2 A term used for *Volksschule* in certain parts of the German Empire.
3 *Selekta* was a special class for outstanding students. It dated back to at least the 17th Century but was in decline by the time Dr. Hammer was writing. See Jens Nagel, "Schulrhetorik an Gymnasien um 1700: Die Öffentlichen Redeakte Zwischen Meritokratie und Repräsentation." *Aufklärung*, vol. 28, 2016, pp. 29–60, at p. 36. JSTOR, <www.jstor.org/stable/26333841>.

visitor. It concerned a "student" (in this region a common term for a seminarist) who had visited her on several occasions, even after eight in the evening. He had "helped her in her studies." But no sexual intercourse took place. The landlady had gossiped about her. She begged the student not to visit her so late. But he did not take any notice. The seminarist left for another seminary. He is long since employed as a teacher. After passing the teacher's exam, which according to her account she passed both in the seminary town where she had the misfortune with the "student," as well in another Rhenish seminary town (in her home district she was refused a position on account of the incident), she took up a position in Paris. She had this position, which paid 40 Francs monthly in addition to free board and lodgings, looking after two children of three and five years old for half a year. The father was a Baron. "He did not work." Instead, he travelled. He was two months in Brussels, two months in Luxembourg, two months in Ostend. Elsa always accompanied him. She boasted that she left, "because she knew French tolerably well, and the children could speak good German." Then she spent a few weeks at home in the small west German town where her mother lived. "But I was not happy at home. The people were too narrow-minded. There you couldn't go out or do anything. And then my mother always reproached me about the student." In the winter, Elsa came to Berlin, at the age of 22. After five months, she ended up in the hospital for prostitutes. "I was everything from on high to maidservant."

 First position: governess for an actress. The husband was a craftsman. During Elsa's time there, the woman never appeared. Elsa received 20 Marks monthly as salary. She had to sleep on the sofa in the dining room. She didn't like that and left after 20 days. She only received 13 Marks salary, as she had broken a milk jug and butter dish.

 Second position: bookkeeper for an engineer in east Berlin. There she received 30 Marks and board and lodgings. After three weeks she left "because the man came to my door at night. Then I should always open." The lock of the connecting door between his room and hers was "broken." Then she placed a suitcase in front of the door. "Then, of course, I immediately gave my notice." He was in his mid-fifties, a widower, childless.

Third position: in the North "at the buffet". She was paid 20 Marks monthly salary. After two days she left. "It just didn't suit me. I couldn't remain with the older lady who served at the buffet. I was not prepared to let such a person boss me about." She left without any pay.

Fourth position: waitress in the vicinity of Alexanderplatz. She received no commission, but tips. It was a café. From one o'clock the entrance was closed. When someone knocked, they were let in. Regular clients socialized there. The manageress said to the waitresses, you are there solely to entertain the clients. The premises had a white lantern. The girls drank with the clients. There was always an enticing prospect, namely the girls themselves. The girls were obliged to stay three paces away from the men. A client, a physician (the address given by Elsa was correct) said: "What do I get out of it when I come here, and you must stay three paces…. That was never so before," and he left. She rented a room from the manageress for 30 Marks monthly. She stayed there for three weeks. Then a man took her away. "He invited me to come after the café. I only had two hours free. At 10 o'clock I had not returned. The man said he wanted to look after me. That I shouldn't go back anymore." That's what Elsa did. "How did you find the manageress?" I asked the girl. "In an advertisement in the *Vossische* newspaper,"[4] she replied:

"Seeking three young ladies from out-of-town, well-educated, preferably with language skills."

When she made her way to the cited address, the woman sent a kind of domestic servant, Elsa should present herself in person. The woman received her in a private room and said she had a business. It was a highly reputable bar, and the girls earned up to 120 Marks a month. The men who frequented the bar were all wealthy. Elsa took the position and had to pay 30 Marks in rent for a room at the woman's, payable in advance. She lived off her savings since she still had to buy food. The anticipated tips of course did not materialise.

---

4   A prominent Berlin newspaper aimed at a liberal middle class readership. Editions from 1848 to 1934 are available online at: <https://zefys.staatsbibliothek-berlin.de/list/title/zdb/27112366/>.

Fifth position: waitress in a big city in central Germany. A Berlin employment agency had told Elsa she could earn in X. from 12 to 13 Marks a day. Elsa travelled in fourth class to X. and reported at the bar, in front of which hung a red lamp. She could start immediately. There she engaged in sexual intercourse, when she had the opportunity, to earn money. Her highest daily earning were five Marks (two men). Tips amounted to at most two Marks a day. A man in general paid three Marks for sexual intercourse. She was always afraid. As a result, sexual intercourse with men produced little. After five days, she travelled to a university town in central Germany as waitress in a restaurant, where she stayed three days. Then she took a man with her to Berlin. They travelled in third class stopping over in X. where Elsa still had some clothes. In X. they lived as man and wife in a hotel. Two days later they arrived in Berlin. The man no longer maintains Elsa. "The man was married. It was all the same. I was back in Berlin." Then Elsa went into a *Mädchenheim* (girl's home)[5] and stayed there one night. The next day it was discovered she was Catholic. Then the nun gave her a sheet of paper full of addresses to which she should apply. Elsa made no use of the addresses, since she would not enter a catholic girl's home, because there she would have to confess, and she wouldn't confess. She preferred prostitution and was arrested in the evening, taken to Alexanderplatz, examined by the resident medical assistant and found to be healthy. She had to sign two papers: "That was a warning."

Sixth position: kitchen maid in a reputable restaurant in Schöneberg.[6] She stated that she had to work until two o'clock at night and was only half-full from the food she was given. For that reason, she left her position after eight days. She also injured her foot. She went to the hospital but could not be admitted. The nurse asked about payment. Elsa said she had lost her pocketbook. A moist bandage was applied, and later she attended an outpatient clinic for treatment.

---

5   In Prussia, in the period 1901–1906, there were an estimated 11,481 young women placed in such homes: see Manfred Kappeller and Sabine Hering, *Eine Einführung zur Geschichte der Kindheit und Jugend im Heim*, Fachhochschule Potsdam, 2017, at pp. 9–10.

6   Until 1920, a self-governing city and then a district of Berlin.

In the same period, she returned to prostitution. The official who had already arrested her once, came across her again but didn't place her under control, because she had applied for a new position in Halensee.[7] "It wasn't true, but I had to say something." Then, sometime later, she was taken from lodgings in the north [of Berlin] and taken to the police headquarters and was transferred for compulsory treatment on account of a purulent discharge. She stated on admittance that she had never been sick before, is above-average height and a radiant appearance, namely a healthy complexion. In the hospital she was consistently cheerful.

Seven siblings died in early childhood, four are still living.

A 24-year-old brother is a master carpenter.

A 16-year-old sister is an apprentice milliner.

A four-year-old sister lives with her mother.

She had her first periods at 16.

Her first sexual intercourse was in Berlin when she was 22. "What the man was, I don't know. I had been here a couple of days. I met him on the street. I was inebriated. We travelled to the Grunewald.[8] Another day, I again went to Grunewald. That was a different man. Then I still had money. Neither paid." In total, Elsa says she has been paid by four men. The traveller who paid her fare, and similar cases, she did not include.

While Elsa was in the hospital, her mother was informed that the city of Berlin wanted to collect from her the costs (2.50 Marks a day). The mother wrote to her daughter, "never come home again, as long as I live."

A religious woman, who is employed with a monthly salary of 50 Marks and as a result visits the hospital twice weekly for about one hour to converse with some of the girls, had offered her a place in a foundation and future employment opportunities.

The girl told me: "I do not know whether I will go to the foundation. The girls all say it can last for six months until you get a position. When I could first go (onto the streets), then look for a position."

---

7   Halensee is a small lake in Berlin.
8   A district of that name in the west of Berlin, including a wooded area.

She then returned to prostitution. Within a few weeks, she was again handed over to the police, this time as a girl placed under the regular control of the vice police.

Her handwriting is simple, regularly spaced. She demonstrates signs of pressure points (thoughtfulness), high "t" horizontal lines (self-confidence), absence of full stops (rash, trusting).

On her admission, she suffered from discharge. Two months after her discharge, she had already contracted a syphilitic rash.

In evaluation of case 5:

Elsa readily engaged in prostitution, even when she was not paid. Therefore, she was not forced into the path of prostitution by penury. "The experience that hunger/often forces young working-class girls/onto the path of vice,"[9] I cannot confirm in the case of Berlin female prostitutes. Not one single girl was placed under vice police control who had not previously had the opportunity to sustain herself by other means, even if only through foundations. If a girl is without work or housing, then the hospitable rooms of the city shelter are open to her. In case of emergency, each police district provides accommodation for the night, until poor relief can be requested. Perhaps the vice police would give effect to my suggestion, whereby each girl that is arrested for the first time is given a booklet with brief information about employment opportunities, the city's shelter, poor relief and foundations.

V. Remarks on Religion and Sexual Life

Between religious ideas and practices on the one hand, and human sexual life on the other, there are manifold connections.

---

[9] "*Die Erfahrung, daß der Hunger/Junge Mädchen aus dem Volke/Auf die Bahn oft drängt des Lasters.*" My trans.) The source of this excerpt of verse, first published in 1888, is the Austrian poet Robert Hamerling (1830–1889). See: Robert Hamerling, *Homunculus. Modernes Epos in zehn Gesäingen.* Second Song, Karl-Maria Gut, 2014, at p. 16; and Ritchie Robertson, "Robert Hamerling and the Survival of Epic." *Austrian Studies*, vol. 16, 2008, pp. 142–53. *JSTOR*, <www.jstor.org/stable/27944881>.

When I attempted many years ago to identify through observation the origins of religious practice, the first thing that struck me was that the vast majority of those going to the Protestant churches in Berlin, insofar as I visited them, were maidens, virginal men, and old women, namely primarily the sexually unsatisfied parts of the populace. When it is also evident that the dominant religious communities promote the limitation of sexual intercourse, then it appears to me conversely that sexual abstinence encourages a susceptibility for religious feelings, and not only for them, but for all thoughts of eternal life. A similar relationship between abstinence and artistic sensibility seems to apply. Marriage ties one to the earthly world, and one who by means of propagation seeks to achieve rejuvenation of part of his body and a longer life often forfeits forces otherwise available for the world of ideas, which seek to elevate one above the earthly world. In other words: religious satisfaction and sexual satisfaction are in mutual (contrary) contradiction. That is the first connection I can determine between religion and sexual life.

The contradiction between religious and sexual satisfaction must have a reason. I consider this reason grounded in the fact that religion offers an alternative to sexual satisfaction.[10] The person who accepts this substitution, cannot accept sexual satisfaction, and the person who accepts sexual

---

10 Dr. Hammer's opinion on this topic may well have been influenced by *Psychopathia Sexualis*, first published by the pioneering German psychiatrist Krafft-Ebing (1840–1902) in 1886: "On the contrary, we find that the sexual instinct, when disappointed and unappeased, frequently seeks and finds a substitute in religion." 12th ed., Heinemann, 1939, at p. 8. This viewpoint cannot be attributed to Freud, since his writings on religion, notably *Obsessive Actions and Religious Practices*, were first published in 1907. Dr. Hammer's views also do not reflect Marx's view that "religion is the opium of the people," expressed in the introduction to *Zur Kritik der Hegelschen Rechtsphilosophie* (1844): see Esther Oluffa Pedersen, "Religion is the Opium of the People: An Investigation into the Intellectual Context of Marx's Critique of Religion." *History of Political Thought*, Vol. 36, No. 2, 2015, pp. 354–87. *JSTOR*, <www.Jstor.Org/Stable/26228603>. Otto Weininger (1880–1903) published *Sex and Character: A Fundamental Investigation* in 1903, a work which does address the relationship between religious views and sexuality, in particular in Chapter XII, "On the Nature of Women."

satisfaction, does not need this substitution. What is the substitution religion offers in exchange for sexual satisfaction?

This substitution varies according to the religious system. In antiquity, it was a sacred revelation, a revelation arising from religious practices.

A section of Christian zealots practiced religious flagellantism, in mutual flagellation with the simultaneous stress of religious aims, the endurance of pain for the purpose of atonement, a substitute for sexual satisfaction.

In modern times, such practices have waned. The absence of sexual satisfaction is still greatly eased through inner spiritual devotion to the fulfilling conceptual world of a higher being. The inner veneration and spiritual devotion to a bridegroom of our souls[11] no longer leaves any place for an inner devotion to a man. The fervent veneration of an angelic virgin stifles the feeling for womanhood suffused with worldly lust.

Strong sensuality and pronounced religious belief converge, so that often the same person is for a period very religious, and then for a period licentious.

Young w[hore], old nun,[12] is a Swiss proverb. The pious can also be found among Berlin prostitutes, so that extreme sensuality interchanges with onsets of fervent religiosity.

In order to influence the girls by religious means, I would emphasise the following points as of importance:

1. A compulsory display of suffering for the purpose of spiritual consolation should be ended.[13] The benefits of religious treatment should not be imposed.

---

11 *"Seelenbräutigam."* For an account of the origin of this phrase, see: Jaroslav Pelikan, "The Bridegroom of the Soul," *Jesus through the Centuries*: His Place in the History of Culture Yale, 1999, pp. 122–32.
12 See for this phrase (*"Junge Hure, alte Betschwester"*): Karl Simrock (editor), *Die deutschen Volksbücher*, H. L. Brönner, 1846, 5th edn., no. 5126, at p. 235.
13 *"Eine zwangsvorführung zwecks Erduldens des geistlichen Zuspruchs hat zu unterbleiben."* It is not specified to which religious practice Dr. Hammer is here referring. *Eine Zwangsvorführung* generally refers to a subpoena in judicial proceedings. *Erduldens*, as well as suffering or enduring, can mean the religious practice of mortification.

2. Spiritual methods should not be confounded with worldly threats. Therefore, it is not permissible to threaten a girl, if she will not enter a foundation, that she will be reported to the police, and thereby placed under supervision. On the contrary, it is permissible for a religious authority to threaten the punishments of hell if the person is convinced of the reality of these punishments.
3. Threats to health should not be addressed by way of spiritual consolation. Expressions of remorse, which can easily degenerate into mental illness, are less worthwhile than good intentions.
4. Serious bodily illness should not be worsened through the eliciting of deep-seated mental distress.
5. Consolation in misfortune, active support through information about municipal employment agencies, reference to the fact that change is possible, strengthening of a sense of purpose through reassuring encouragement, these are all elements of primary importance to be taken account of by religious men and women who bring spiritual assistance to establishments for prostitutes.

6 Frida Schlecht

(No. 100 in my files)

Protestant religion, born in wedlock.

The vice police handed over Frida Schlecht for compulsory treatment at the age of 14.

She is the daughter of a coachman, who was seriously ill when Frida last saw him.

Her present mother is a cleaning lady, also does washing.

She can't remember when exactly she left school. She had completely stopped school attendance by the age of thirteen and a half.

She was discharged, "because the school principal said I was a bad influence on the other children."

Most recently, Frida had stolen.

Even during her school days, she was "never at home."

"I didn't want to stay at home! Then I took up with men."

"From the age of 13, I was with men."

"Since the age of thirteen and a half I stopped going to school, thrown out of IV. Class."[1]

About her first sexual intercourse, she admitted she ran away from her parents and had gone missing for three days. What did she live on? "When my friends gave me something, I took it."

What sort of friends where they? "Her name was S., she still went to school. Her father was dead. Her mother was a caretaker." What did they give you? "Bread." Where did you spend the night? "Either on stairways or

---

[1] In general, a *Volksschule* had eight classes for each year of attendance, but this number varied widely both regionally and according to the resources of the school: see: Marion Klewitz, "Preußische Volksschule vor 1914. Zur regionalen Auswertung der Schulstatistik. *Zeitschrift für Pädagogik,* vol. 27, no. 4, 1981, pp. 551–73.

taken away by men." Where did you sleep when you were taken away, before you had sexual intercourse with men? "Slept on the floor everywhere."

After she had wandered the streets for three days, she went early at 6 in the morning to the west of Berlin.

About her first sexual intercourse, she said: "He took me straight away and laid me onto the stairway." "He didn't pay anything." "I never told anybody." "Then once a man propositioned[2] me in the street. A friend of my father saw us. Then we …. Then the friend told my father he had seen me with a man."

Frida has been working regularly as a prostitute for the last two months, "taken it up straightaway."

Once she was paid two Marks; nothing more. "Since then, I have not been paid anything."

With whom then have you had sexual intercourse?

"They were gentlemen acquaintances."

What sort of gentlemen?

"They aren't gentlemen anymore." "At a bar." "I was taken to a dive.[3] There they gave me as much to eat as I wanted." From the dive, she was taken back home by the police. I stayed one night at home and then left. Why?

"I couldn't stay at home."

Why?

"My father kicked me and hit me with his fist. He punched me and laid me on the sofa and for at least a quarter of an hour hit me around the head."

Once again, Frida left.

Then she associated with men she only knew by their criminal nicknames.

"Frankfurter Lude."

"General."

"Suppler."

"Streichler."

"Magiarenfritze."[4]

2   The German word "*rangekriecht*" is a slang expression.
3   *Kaschemme*, translated here as dive, is a term for a thieves' den or doss house.
4   "*Luder*" was a common word for pimp; "*Suppler*" may be an alternative spelling of "*Kuppler*," a pimp; "*Streichler*" means a flatterer; "*fritze*" is a pejorative slang word attached to a description of a man – "*Magiaren*" may refer to a Magyar. The use of

Frida Schlecht

Frankfurter Lude went begging in an eastern suburb of Berlin. He told Frida to wait for him in a dive. He then went with her to the dive and there onto the floor. There sexual intercourse took place. The General also had sexual intercourse with her. When Frankfurter Lude left, a man came and took her back to the dive. The General was in the dive and took the girl into the washroom. "I didn't want to with him. I certainly said something. But afterwards they didn't even ask. They just force you."

In this manner she continued with her experiences.

On another occasion, she stole 75 Marks. "A friend, a schoolgirl, had a position. I went with her. They knew that I was never at home. They took pity on me. I stayed there for two nights. It was in a *Mädchenkneipe*. My friend was there to do the washing. I helped with the washing and everything. There I stole 75 Marks from the linen cupboard in the parlour."

The night after, she went out with Suppler, bought clothing, a hat, the lot, spent 15 Marks on eating and drinking in a dance hall. Then she was drunk. "Money, everything went." At the end, she still had about 10 Marks.

Then they were both arrested. Suppler was placed in custody. Frida in the hospital for prostitutes.

She told me that an 18-year-old brother works with a farmer; a 17-year-old brother is a milk deliveryman in Berlin. "He should have been punished. He broke into a cellar. He received a warning at the age of 14. He speaks ill of me: I have to say that about him. When he sees me, then he always beats me, bloodies all my teeth and nose." Furthermore, Frida admitted that, at the time she was already engaged in sexual intercourse with other men, he had indecently touched her. Their beds were next to each other.

A 10-year-old sister is at a *Gemeindeschule*. A 7-year-old stepsister is from the second mother.

"Nonetheless, I have a second mother. My first mother died five years ago from a heart condition, an enlarged liver, and tapeworm."

When did you have your second mother?

"A few weeks later."

---

criminal nicknames is reflected in the novels *Die Tigerin* (1925) by Walter Serner (1913–1942), set in the Parisian underworld, and *Berlin Alexanderplatz* (1929) by Alfred Döblin (1878–1957).

Frida is poorly developed, has never had periods, has put on weight during her care in the hospital. Although she was put in a ward in with "decent" persons, she secretly managed to start a lesbian relationship with a girl from another floor.

Her handwriting is uneducated.

In assessment: Frida is a born criminal. Her brother also has a criminal disposition, in that he committed a burglary at 14 years old. The principal of the *Gemeindeschule* that she attended informed me that a mass of documents about her are held by the guardianship court. Also, certain cranial characteristics of an innate criminal in the sense of the Lombrosian method were recognizable at first sight.[5] Her early developed sensuality drove her after a few weeks of enforced sexual abstinence to lesbian love.

VI. Criminality and Prostitution

An act punishable with death, hard labour camp (*Zuchthaus*), or imprisonment for more than five years is a felony (*Verbrechen*)[6] (the German Penal Code).[7]

Without doubt, prostitutes are not criminals in this sense.

---

5 Cesare Lombroso (1835–1909) was an Italian criminologist. See Mariacarla Gadebusch Bondio, "From the "Atavistic" to the "Inferior" Criminal Type: The Impact of the Lombrosian Theory of the Born Criminal on German Psychiatry." *Criminals and their Scientists: The History of Criminology in International Perspective*, edited by Peter Becker and Richard F. Wetzell, Cambridge UP, 2006, pp. 183–206.

6 Under German penal law a *Verbrechen* is to be distinguished from a *Vergehen*, which is a category of offence (*Delikt*) with a lesser punishment.

7 The German Penal Code was adopted in 1900. A *Zuchthaus* was a harsher form of imprisonment than a prison with forced labour. On proposals to abolish the *Zuchthaus*, see: W. Mittermaier, "Abschaffung Des Zuchthauses." *Deutsche Rechts-Zeitschrift*, vol. 5, no. 8, 1950, pp. 174–76. *JSTOR*, <www.jstor.org/stable/20810587>.

Lay people, in particular doctors, primarily understand by criminals those who in order to attain their own advantage act selfishly to an exaggerated extent without consideration for their fellow men.

Scientists speak in these circumstances of an exaggerated development of egoistical, self-serving tendencies in opposition to those drives that are social and benefit the collectivity.

Also, from these perspectives, it is not permissible in my opinion to treat prostitutes as criminals. So long as the overwhelming majority of menfolk who are not counted as criminals are actively engaged in the trade of prostitutes, so long as society through the police authorities issue regulations which proscribe that the trade of prostitution should be steered into specified channels, I consider it inadmissible that a girl should be individually reproached when she pursues this officially supervised trade. Only those men who themselves do not engage in sexual intercourse with prostitutes may be morally entitled to pass unfavourable judgments on prostitutes. Only those women, in my opinion, should be allowed to make harsh judgments are those who at the same time treat a man's sexual intercourse with a prostitute with contempt. Such women at least think logically. But they are rarely to be found, since they would in most cases be forced to recognize that all sexual intercourse with men would have to be abandoned, including sexual intercourse with their fathers, brothers, husbands.

Therefore, I am opposed to the common usage of prostitutes being classed as criminals:

1. On legal grounds.
2. On moral grounds.
3. On grounds of the following logical reasoning.

I am much more inclined to treat both prostitutes and other women differently according to criminality: a) criminal women; b) non-criminal women; hence: a) criminal prostitutes; b) non-criminal prostitutes.

Criminal prostitutes are thieves, fraudsters, swindlers, blackmailers, who alongside or in support of their criminality also engage in prostitution.

Non-criminal prostitutes are those girls who engage in prostitution within the confines of the legal regulations.

I distinguish the concept of criminality from that of sin; since, according to the present day dominant Christian viewpoint, all prostitutes as such are to be counted as sinners, but self-evidently are also all men who consort with them to be treated as sinners.

I cannot, therefore, verify the assertion by the Lombrosian school of thought, that prostitutes are mostly physically degenerated, since until now I have not had the opportunity thoroughly to check thousands of healthy girls for "signs of degeneration." It is rare for healthy girls to come to the doctors, nearly always those who are sick. There is presently no investigation of the whole female population in the manner of that of all German males conducted under the authority of military examinations. That is why I consider it valuable first to set out these ten lives. I have noted when I have observed an exceptional intensity or cluster of signs of degeneration. Thus, immediately upon the handing over of Frida Schlecht, even before I had examined her file, I could form the strong suspicion that it was *delinquente nata,* a case of innate criminality.

7 Gretchen Früh

(No. 103 in my files)

Born in wedlock, seventeen years old, Jewish. My medical assistant brought a seventeen-year-old girl in from outside the Fröbelstrasse,[1] dressed in bloomers and the cheap, short-lived clothing of the priestesses of free, but paid, love, who was suffering terrible pains at every step. A person with fever accompanied by purulent urethritis resulting from infection with gonorrhoea[2] suffers terrible pain, and yet she refused admission into a hospital because she came from welfare training and was afraid to be sent back.

Gretchen is from a big city in central Germany. Both her parents are alive and run a wholesale business.

She has four brothers. They are:

1. a 28-year-old married photographer in the west of Germany, who is father of three children;
2. a 19-year-old wheelwright;
3. a 13-year-old in *Gymnasium*;[3]
4. a 9-year-old in a *Bürgerschule*.[4]

---

1 The street in which Dr. Hammer's clinic was located.
2 **Gonorrhoea**: A venereal disease caused by the bacterium Gonococcus. Within two to ten days after infection the first symptoms – painful and frequent urination and discharge from the urethra or vagina- may appear. Dr. A. S. Playfair, *supra*, at p. 110.
3 Secondary schools in this period were broadly divided into *Gymnasium*, *Realgymnasium* and *Oberrealschule*. These schools prepared pupils for the *Abitur* examination guaranteeing admission to university education: Fritz K. Ringer, "Higher Education in Germany in the Nineteenth Century." *Journal of Contemporary History*, vol. 2, no. 3, 1967, pp. 123–38, at pp. 128–30. *JSTOR*, <www.jstor.org/stable/259810>.
4 *Bürgerschule* had a more practically orientated curriculum and generally aimed at pupils who were not set to progress to secondary school. The complex organisation

Her three sisters are:

1. a thirty-year-old, a married woman who emigrated to America, who is in a childless marriage for ten years;
2. a 24-year-old wife of a travelling salesman and mother of two children;
3. a 6-year-old sister, who lives with her parents.

From the age of 6 until 14, she attended the *Bürgerschule* of her hometown, without repeating a year; and then a year at female teacher training college.[5] She had to leave because she was pregnant. She spent four weeks in the hospital of her hometown. Then she came to the Jewish Reformatory[6] in Berlin. Her baby was born in Berlin. She nourished her for a quarter of a year. "They wanted to take away the child." Then she jumped out of the window and broke both legs. Afterwards, she was in hospital for ten weeks. From there, she stayed in lodgings with a teacher near the Rhine. Five weeks later she moved out. She travelled back to her parents with her savings. Her mother chided her and said she should not prostitute herself. Then she was sent to an aunt in London. "Because I couldn't bear the climate, I returned to my parents." She stayed four days at home. Her mother remonstrated with her. She could not go out. Then she travelled back to Berlin. For two weeks she was an extra in a theatre for 45 Marks

---

of the various categories of schools operating in Prussia in the late 19th century, and the role of the higher *Bürgerschule* in the transition between primary and secondary education, is examined by Hans-Jürgen Apel, and Michael Klöcker, "Die preußische höhere Bürgerschule im Vormärz. Analyse des Bildungsprogramms und der Schülerschaft an der ersten rheinischen höheren Bürgerschule zu Köln." *Zeitschrift für Pädagogik,* vol. 30, no. 6, 1984, pp. 775–95.

5   A *Lehrerinnenseminar* were educational institutes that prepared girls for careers as teachers either in primary or secondary schools for girls: see Huerkamp, Claudia. "Jüdische Akademikerinnen in Deutschland 1900–1938." *Geschichte Und Gesellschaft,* vol. 19, no. 3, 1993, pp. 311–31, at p. 316. *JSTOR,* <www.jstor.org/stable/40185665>.

6   This may be a reference to the *Jüdische Waisenhaus* in Prenzlauerberg founded in 1833 by Baruch Auerbach (1793–1864). See for a history: <www.pankow-weissen see-prenzlauerberg.berlin/de/juedisches-waisenhaus-prenzlauer-berg>.

a month. Then for three weeks she prostituted herself. She came to me with gonorrhoea.

1. Periods at 13.
2. Sexual intercourse at 14.

"There was an officer (in her hometown). We lived near the riding school. I stayed with him for eight days. My parents concluded I had had an accident and published it in the newspaper. After eight days, I went back quite unashamed."

"The second was with a relative. I had sexual intercourse with him three times. I got pregnant with him."

"Then I had sexual intercourse with a doctor in the clinic."

"None of them paid."

"Recently I have been working as a prostitute. I had a room in the students' district for 6 Marks daily."

The girl is 162 cm tall, had 54 cm maximum head circumference, she still has scars from a suicide attempt (cutting of an artery).

She states her father is extraordinarily strict, as is her mother; she is terribly unlucky, so that she would prefer to die, but she cannot and must not do it, as she has obligations to fulfil towards her child.

Her handwriting is sloping. The T-joints are poorly developed. The stem strokes go off in every direction (completely confused, flaccid character).

In assessment: This is a girl who when she reached the age of puberty was dissatisfied. Unstable and dissatisfied, she travelled through Germany and to England. She did not have the good fortune to adjust to a life of sexual abstinence. Her adjustment mostly manifested itself in regular masturbation, so far as my observations suffice. She also never had the opportunity to form a lasting relationship. And thus she came to grief.

VII. On the Sexual Enlightenment of Adolescents

Nowadays, you frequently hear that it is the duty of parents to enlighten their growing children about sexual life. This enlightenment presents difficulties that are often overlooked. In most cases only formal difficulties are acknowledged. Whole books have been written to help address these reputedly significant problems. To this end, similarities with the plant kingdom are employed. To this end, use of the most subtle hints is advised, to avoid arousing shameful feelings. Highly detailed trial lessons are placed into the hands of parents, but those points on which, in my opinion, such enlightenment mostly fails, are scarcely touched upon.

The main point is not to rid sexually mature young men and women from the fairy-tale of the stork nor to clarify that copulation and fertilization are required to create a human being, but it is mainly a question of instilling firm moral principles.

But how can parents provide effective enlightenment if they themselves lack clarity? But how can clarity be demanded of lay persons on points about which educated persons of every age and nation have for decades rigorously debated without reaching a generally accepted solution?

Should the father tell his son: my dear son, live in celibacy until marriage? Or should he tell him: if you live in celibacy, then as a rule you will lapse into masturbation. Should he on being asked, tell him how he practices it, or should he withhold this information, or should he lie to his son?

Honesty and veracity are hardly to be insisted upon if sexual enlightenment is coming from the parents. It is in any event straightforward for pious and strongly religious people. They can simply refer to a biblical passage from the New Testament or to the word of God, and the matter is settled both for them and their devout children. The non-believing majority will, however, have a less pleasing outcome.

If the parents stick to the truth, then enlightenment could run as follows:

1. Health aspects.

Sexual intercourse in the age of sexual maturity invigorates the body; through intercourse between two healthy persons, the occurrence of venereal disease is impossible. Sexual celibacy is on medical grounds harmful and unharmful. There are proponents for both opinions.

With good care and a healthy physique, pregnancy is beneficial to a woman. There are means to prevent pregnancy.

2. Legal aspects.

If a woman gives herself to her lover outside marriage, she is treated as debased. A teacher, for example, loses her position. Public opinion, that power which often is not surpassed by the fickleness of a lover, by the brutality of a medieval executioner, by the arrogant importunity of a jester, this public opinion at times tramples the girl, that is a mother to be, into the dirt, while it simply makes fun of the paramour. A person who does not pay attention to public opinion, runs the risk of growing lonely or being destroyed.

3. Ethical aspects.

It is considered immoral to have extra-marital intercourse or to prevent pregnancy.

4. Personal aspects.

We as parents have not ourselves practiced that which we have required of you children. But for you it is best to follow our words and not our deeds.

This must be acknowledged by most parents of our homeland, if they wish to combine their enlightenment with honesty and veracity, and if they would have the trust of their children in sexual matters, and if they wish to answer their questions honestly.

A few pious parents, those who base themselves on religious grounds, the names of which nearly everyone recognises, can certainly honestly and truthfully give the following answers:

"Through vigour and in the belief of fulfilling a commandment of God, we have managed to lead an abstemious life. With religious exercises ('with the help of Jesus' says a Protestant evangelist), we overcome self-gratification. Thus, we are delivered into a happy marriage."

For this reason, enlightenment by those who are free of grounds for self-reproach can be effective. The rest often do well not to touch upon this domain, in which in most cases they are in any event not trusted by their developing children.

I consider the parents' good example as more effective than fine words of enlightenment.

8 Hulda Schnell

(No. 9 in my files)

20 years-old, of Protestant religion, born in wedlock, in a large city in Saxony.

Father is alive and healthy, a self-employed stonemason and foreman.

Mother is alive and healthy.

Four dead siblings. Two male twins died at a very young age. Two girls also died young. They could hardly walk.

A 22-year-old brother, currently a soldier, was foreman in a carpentry workshop.

An 18-year-old brother is mason and works with his father.

A 16-year-old brother is frail. He has a lip fissure and a cleft palate; he also once broke his arm. Hilda is of the opinion: "He is cleverer than us but cannot express himself. He will perhaps be a clerk. Now he is at home and is a worry for my mother."

A 9-year-old brother attends the local *Bürgerschule*.[1]

A 30-year-old unmarried sister wanted to marry. "But it was a man of higher rank. He worked at the *Kreishauptmannschaft*.[2] His aunt did not allow the marriage, because the sister didn't have enough money. Now he is in the lunatic asylum. She had three children with him. One is with the mother. One was taken by the paternal grandmother. The other is with a foster family. The sister pays them. She works as a washerwoman; he pays nothing."

---

1 For the development of *Bürgerschule* in the primary school system in Saxony, see: Roland Schmidt, "Schulgeschichte der sachsischen vogtlandes." http://schulgeschichte.de/index.html.

2 *Kreishauptmannschaft* acted as an administrative tribunal in Saxony: see D. Tolmitt, "Geschichte der Verwaltungsgerichtsbarkeit in Sachsen." *Handbuch der Geschichte der Verwaltungsgerichtsbarkeit in Deutschland und Europa*, edited by Karl-Peter Sommermann and Bert Schaffarzik, Springer, 2019, pp. 593–629, at pp. 605–06.

A second sister is 24-years-old and unmarried; she makes stockings for a stocking manufacturer: "she is childless but is in a relationship. She is very respectable. She wouldn't surrender herself until she is married."

A 13-year-old lives at home and attends *Bürgerschule*.

Hulda attended the *Bezirksschule*[3] from the age of 6 until 14. She repeated classes several times. The only childhood illness she could recall having was diphtheria. In second class she was confirmed.

At 14, she served as cook for her landlord for 6 Marks monthly. After one and a half years she left: "She wanted to better herself and leave."

After, she was a housemaid with a widow of a railway foreman for 12 Marks monthly. She stayed there for two years. Then she changed position, because the woman left the city with her daughters.

Afterwards, she learnt to cook and for 18 months she worked in a hotel. "My mother took me away. I had to learn dressmaking. I had also met my husband there. He was a waiter in the hotel. I told that to my mother, that it had caused quite a stir."

Then she learnt dressmaking.

"My brother paid for that; it didn't cost much as it was with relatives." For six months she stayed in her hometown. Then she married and went to Berlin with her husband. "Since then, I haven't worked any longer; I always had enough money to live on."

1. Periods at 18.
2. Sexual intercourse with her present husband at 19, half-a-year before her marriage.

She hasn't ever had a child, nor aborted, nor a stillbirth. Her husband works as a waiter in sleeping cars. He has 4 days work; 2 days free; 2 days work; 2 days free; 4 days work. He earns 40 Marks a month as well as tips. He has rented for his wife a three-room apartment in the west of Berlin. Exactly six weeks after her marriage she was handed over to the vice police.

---

3   A primary school in the local district (*Bezirk*) supervised by the *Bezirksschulinspektor*. See Roland Schmidt, *supra*, "Die Ersten Bezirksschulinspektoren im Vogtland."

She said: "I wrote him a letter in my apartment. It is hopefully lying there in front of the door."

Is that of any use?

"When he sees me, it will help. He likes me a lot."

Concerning her misfortune, she said as follows:

"We once went to eat at Aschinger.[4] That was just once, since my husband had to leave again straightaway. There I got to know a woman, while my husband was there. We arranged to meet up. We did not go. My husband said: You shouldn't go there. It doesn't seem to me the right path to take."

Why did you nonetheless go?

"I had nothing to do, absolutely nothing. Then I went to .... Street No. ... (quartier latin)[5] and we chatted until 8 o'clock in the evening. Then a number of girls arrived and brought men along. The woman said: You should take one as well. I took one there. There was a better man with him. The man was on the Chausseestrassse.[6] He offered me a cup of coffee. I didn't accept. We went for a walk. Round the block. I didn't think anything of it. I otherwise have a cold nature. Then we went upstairs. Scarcely were we up there when a police officer arrived. He called me an impertinent, filthy whore. He dragged me to the police station. There they brought out a girl who was under control. She said she had seen me go up. The female doctor examined me, said nothing. I was placed back into the cell. The next day I was taken to the doctor, and from there to the Fröbel hospital."

Hulda had a lesion in her mouth, which had a distant resemblance to syphilis. After ten days' treatment, without a syphilitic cure being necessary, she was released cured. During this time, she received no answer from her husband. He also didn't recover her apartment keys.

---

4   Aschinger was a restaurant and dance hall in Berlin in Bülowstraße near the Friedrichstrasse railway station.

5   A district in Berlin centred on Die Elsässer Straße, (the present Torstraße between Rosenthaler Platz and Oranienburger Tor) which at the time was reputed for its variety shows. See: "17. Kinos, Danz und Varieté." <https://www.berlinstreet.de/brunnenstrasse/brunnen17>. Accessed 6 April 2021.

6   A street in the middle of Berlin.

The handwriting is strongly inclined (143°). A tendency to sudden pressure points is present (sensuality). The full stop is missing (imprudence).

Evaluation: Hulda has a brother, who suffers from a learning difficulty, a sister who gave birth three times out-of-wedlock, and she herself more than once repeated class. She therefore probably already in her childhood showed evidence of lacking sufficient endurance and energy, although she may also have been reasonably gifted. Her husband is probably laid low from the presently circulating public morality, which treats significantly differently the wife and the lover, the man and the woman. The lack of meaningful work and the absence of her husband have aroused her sensual excitability. At first, she just wanted to take a look. She considered herself capable of stepping back at any moment. Even so she still had the strength to refuse the money offered to her. She acknowledged that the man left money on the table, from where the landlady may have taken it.

VIII. The Male World and Prostitution

There are multiple reasons why men frequent prostitutes.

Although every young man in a large city should be able to form a long-term relationship, if he so wishes, which does not cost him anything, we can see that the majority of men from every social class, in most cases until they catch a venereal disease, consort with prostitutes.

Accordingly, there are two notable points: 1. The rejection of sexual abstinence. 2. The choice of prostitutes.

> 1. In my opinion, the rejection of sexual abstinence is mainly because young people at first-hand experience abstinence disorders. Feelings of loneliness, the agonies of solitude lead them to sexual intercourse. They want to escape the ties of masturbation. They do not want to become incapable of copulation. Since they are afraid of the spectre of male weakness and are afraid of becoming permanently incapable of sexual intercourse, they try, if they have reached such a low point, to be able to achieve that their sexual

organs[7] are no longer in the necessary condition for copulation.[8] Since many experience that without sexual intercourse they constantly fall back on masturbation with its pitiful consequences, they seek to bring about regular sexual intercourse. At the same time, they are constantly encouraged by so-called reputable ladies to engage in intercourse with prostitutes, finally they succumb to these suggestions.

2. Intercourse with prostitutes rather than voluntary relationships are chosen:

a) since many young men believe that prostitutes cannot be corrupted, and they want to avoid the feelings of guilt arising from seduction of a young woman;

b) since there are municipal authorities that recognise and supervise prostitution, they are as a result convinced that sexual intercourse with prostitutes is harmless and morally permissible for men. The same opinions are supported by customs in the military;

c) intercourse is accessible at any time and results in no future obligations;

d) men often have limited capacity to resist invitations from prostitutes;

e) prostitution enables the satisfaction of perversions. Thus, a person with sickness insurance (*Kassenkranker*)[9] can have

---

[7] Dr. Hammer uses the expression *"Unterleibsorgane,"* which is technically the abdominal organs.

[8] It is difficult to translate this sentence. Dr. Hammer seems to be saying, in a roundabout way, that some men are so afraid of the consequences of masturbation that they refrain, to the detriment of their ability to copulate, presumably by no longer being able to achieve an erection. Instillation of the deleterious consequence of masturbation, both on religious and medical grounds, was widespread at the time. See, for example: Hermann Rohleder, *Die Masturbation*, Rietz, 1898. archive.org/details/diemasturbationeoorohl/mode/2up.

[9] *Kassenkranker* is a person entitled to health insurance reimbursement. The health insurance system was introduced into Imperial Germany by Bismark in 1883. On reimbursement for obligatory treatment for venereal diseases, see: J. Heller and G. Sticker, *Die Haut- und Geschlechtskrankheiten in Staats-, Straf-, Zivil- und Sozialrecht: Entwurf einer Geschichte der Ansteckenden Geschlechtskrankheiten*.

sexual intercourse with three girls in one night. Lovers of pain (sadists and masochists) as well as followers of sexual refinements are often clients of prostitutes.

Springer, 1931, at pp. 81–82. Dr. Hammer through his experience as a travelling doctor formed trenchant views on abuses of the sickness reimbursement regime: see: Jazbinsek, *supra*, at pp. 56–57.

9 Ida Hauptmann

(No. 20 in my files)

Twenty-two-year-old captain's daughter, Protestant religion, born in wedlock. Born in a large city in southern Germany. Her father is an editor and retired captain, her mother is a certified teacher for *Bürgerschule* and higher *Töchterschulen*.[1]

Siblings: a brother died, aged five weeks old.

A 20-year-old sister is a pupil at the art academy and develops designs for a factory.

A 15-year-old and a 13-year-old sister attend the *Töchterschule*.

When Ida was 6, her father retired as captain. He became a writer.

From 6 until 10 years old, she attended Middle School (*Mittelschule*).[2] Then she was sent as a boarder to England until the age of 14. From 14 to 16-years-old she attended the *Elekta* of a higher Berlin *Töchterschule*.

Afterwards, she studied photography for a year. There she earned 3 marks a week.

She couldn't continue as she was short-sighted and enrolled at a private business school for a three-month course at 50 Marks a month. There she learnt short-hand (Stolze-Schrey),[3] typing and bookkeeping.

---

[1] A category of secondary school for girls. An example of a catholic higher *Töchterschule* founded in 1864 in Dortmund by the Congregation of the Sisters of Charity is given by Chamberlain, *supra*, at p. 470.

[2] The *Mittelschule* was a category of school developed in Prussia under the 1872 school reforms and had a more advanced curriculum than the parallel existing *Volksschule*. See: Günter Höffken, *Zur Institutionalisierung und Entwicklung der Mittelschule in Preußen 1872 bis 1945 unter besonderer Berücksichtigung des Chemieunterricht*, PhD thesis, U. of Potsdam, 2006, at pp. 25–29. See also: Zymek, *supra*, at p. 500.

[3] A system of shorthand, a combination of the methods developed by Wilhelm Stolze (1798–1867) and Ferdinand Schrey (1850–1938).

She then worked as correspondent, first in Berlin for nine months, for 75 Marks a month, then in the west of our fatherland for 90 Marks a month. After three-and-a-half weeks, in a heated discussion, she slapped her boss in the face. Then she had a temporary position for several days in the Rhine region. In seven days, she earnt 35 marks. Then she was hired by the same firm at 90 Marks a month. She stayed in this position for over a year. Then she got a position in Berlin for 110 Marks a month, which she again had to give up. She then travelled for a publicity firm and was paid commission only, 30 to 40 Marks a month.

She lost her virginity on her eighteenth birthday. This liaison started through a meeting at an association. "I am not even angry about it; since I would have been much more anxious if it hadn't happened. Shortly before, I had my first nervous convulsions." Ida had sexual intercourse for three years with a student in geotechnology and agricultural land management. He was then employed by a company of international standing in the west of Germany. Since she had once missed her periods, the student accompanied her to a doctor. He examined her and said she would not bear children.

"I would have liked to slap the louse." Since Professor .... (a well-known neurologist) had according to her at the time of an examination told her parents: only childbirth[4] could save her. She was not present but had nonetheless heard his words through the door. She attributed her infertility to the fact that once as member of a gymnastics association she had fallen from a height while climbing a ladder ... She lost her position as a travelling commission agent ... "Then, because I was ashamed to admit to my mother that I had no position, I embarked on the immoral way of life." As she entered the thoroughfare,[5] a man approached and addressed her: young woman, come with me. I am a police officer.[6] Then he took out

---

4   Dr. Hammer uses the phrase *"ein Kindbett"* which is an older version of the term *Wochenbett* and generally refers to postpartum or the period immediately following birth.
5   Dr. Hammer uses the term *"in der Passage ging"*. For the connection between prostitution and the main thoroughfares in Berlin in the mid-19th century, see: Carl Röhrmann, *Der sittliche Zustand von Berlin nach Aufhebung der gedulteten Prostitution des weiblichen Geschlechts*. Röhrmann, 1847, at p. 48.
6   A *kriminalschutzmann* was a police constable in a police section responsible for criminal matters. At the time, the police were separately organised into different

his badge. At the police headquarters, she was examined by the assistant nurse, found to be ill, presented to the doctor, transferred to the Fröbel clinic. She had a seriously neglected syphilis with discharge and could only be released after 66 days of treatment. She said that, apart from her anxiety, she had never, apart from this treatment, been seriously ill. However, she is short-sighted (glasses: approximately 4.5 dioptres). Her mother's are approximately 13.3 dioptres. Her grandmother, aunt, uncle on her mother' side are also short-sighted. Her father is in the past two years "far-sighted" (probably presbyopic).[7] She is not insignificantly hysterical. She had her first onset just before her eighteenth birthday.

Her handwriting inclines from upper left to bottom right.

In England, she says she was operated on both eyes (squint surgery?).[8] Because of her anxiety, she allowed herself to be treated on several occasions, e.g., including with cold water.

About nine months after her discharge, a female friend of mine informed me that she was married to a doctor.

In assessment: The principal factors are a significant impediment in her visual acuity,[9] difficulty in adapting herself to those circles, which she often refers to as the better sort, and a nervous disposition. The young woman does not feel at ease in upper-class circles (representation),[10] concealing her

---

areas of competence: such as the *Sittenpolizei* (vice police), *Marktpolizei* (market police), *Baupolizei* (building police). See: Richard J. Evans, and Andreas Etges. "Polizei, Politik und Gesellschaft in Deutschland 1700–1933." *Geschichte und Gesellschaft*, vol. 22, no. 4, 1996, pp. 609–28, at p. 611. *JSTOR*, <www.jstor.org/stable/40185919>.

7 "**Presbyopia:** Reduction in the power to focus the eyes fully in old age." A. S. Playfair, *supra*, at p. 187.
8 "**Squint Failure:** of the eyes to point in the same direction, caused by a defect in one or more muscles which move the eyeballs." Ibid, at p. 218.
9 "**Visual acuity:** sharpness of vision; the ability to see clearly." Ibid. at p. 249.
10 "Repräsentation: an einem gehobenene gesellschaftlichen Status orienterte, auf Wirkung nach außen bedachter, aufwendiger [Lebens]stil;" ("Representation: an extravagant [life]style oriented towards an elevated social status, preoccupied with outward effect;" my trans.) *Deutsches Universalwörterbuch*, Dudenverlag, 1983, at p. 1028.

suffering from the outside world. This mania for representation[11] in these circles often goes so far that the husband keeps up appearances in front of his wife. In this case, the daughter kept up appearances vis-à-vis her mother. To the question, why she had not become a teacher, Ida replied: mother said: anything else, but not that.

IX. Benefits and Harms of Prostitution

The following principal points may be indicated as beneficial consequences of prostitution:

1. Prostitutes satisfy the all-powerful male sexual drive.
2. Prostitutes by surrendering themselves protect the (so-called) decent girls from extra-marital sexual intercourse.

Point 1: In my opinion, it is an error that prostitutes satisfy the all-powerful male sexual drive.

The release that can be achieved through prostitutes is a release of the crudest sensuality. Even if many prostitutes make every effort, by means of loving, friendly, and cloying ways, to also satisfy the idealistic drives[12] – it is on this very ability to free the young man from the feeling of loneliness that their custom depends – they are only preparing the ground for fresh agonies. Since they inflict the agonies of jealousy on a man, who is also looking for idealistic satisfaction, after a few hours of pleasurable lovemaking. Many of my male acquaintances suffered terribly from these

---

11 "Repräsentationswut" – this expression is often used in the context of ostentatious display or extravagance, for example in the context of baroque art.

12 Dr. Hammer uses the term "*idealen Triebe.*" This may reflect the deep-seated religious connotations that the concept of love engendered. See: Edward Mathieu, "The Christian Love of the German Middle Class: Thuringia, 1870–1912." *German Studies Review*, vol. 34, no. 2, 2011, pp. 305–24. *JSTOR*, <www.jstor.org/stable/41303733>.

conflicts. A thirty-year-old businessman suffered from bitter deception because for a long time he failed to grasp that the professionally bestowed, loving delights of a young woman in a whorehouse were only available so long as he paid. He didn't receive the slightest trifle without paying and for good measure the girl ridiculed him.

The proposition that it is scarcely possible to satisfy basic sexual instincts alone without also satisfaction of idealistic drives, is contradicted by those prostitutes who simply surrender their body. In order to offer males something extra, prostitutes resort to extravagant means of enticement. Thus, one can say that prostitutes arouse males many times but provide only minimal satisfaction.

Second proposition: In my opinion, the second proposition, that prostitutes by their prostitution protect the (so-called) decent girls from extra-marital sexual intercourse, is also false. Certainly, many men seek to satisfy themselves for a time through sexual intercourse with prostitutes. The common result is not the release of sexual impulses, but venereal disease. Following a cure, which is moreover often not complete, those who have had this warning enter into a relationship or get married. If the only alternative was between marriage and prostitution, prostitution would certainly by the pathway of infection often lead to marriage. But as it is, prostitution leads to infection and often to unrestricted extra-marital intercourse.

The principal harms caused by prostitutes are as follows:

1. Prostitutes take money from young men;
2. Prostitutes seduce men into intercourse;
3. Prostitutes spread venereal diseases.

The first point is not completely correct. It is not a particular characteristic of prostitutes to take money from men, rather the (so-called) reputable girls are in many cases in money matters not to be distinguished from prostitutes.[13] In both situations, there are girls with modest and girls with elevated financial demands.

---

13 On the hostile reaction by feminists to Dr. Hammer's views on this point, see: Jazbinsek, *supra*, at pp. 36–37.

In Berlin, there are prostitutes who offer themselves for 25 Pfennigs. I myself, early one morning in 1900 while returning from a birth in the south of our capital city, was addressed by girls drowning each other out with more or less the following words: sex[14] for 50 Pfennigs, sex for 50 Pfennigs, while snowflakes drifted through the air. A married, 56-year-old manual worker told me that he had gone for a midday walk with three colleagues, when all four had met one and the same girl and each paid 50 Pfennigs. The consequences for him were the usual. He caught gonorrhoea as an extra.

On the other hand, there are girls in the large dancehalls who will not go for less than 20 Marks and "a hundred Marks is easily taken there."

Even so, as with prostitutes, there are (so-called) respectable women who are modest in their demands, and women who make heftier demands on the man's wallet. Indeed, (so-called) respectable women may take it for granted that a young man out on a walk should pay for her, since he can call such an exquisite beauty his own, while the (so-called) respectable women at times forget to show their gratitude and consider it to be self-evident that the man should pay for them.

Point 2: Prostitutes frequently seduce male youth into intercourse. But, in my experience, prostitutes are often and efficiently supported in this initiation by "reputable" womankind. Since the so-called reputable women are enthusiastic supporters of double moral standards and contemptuous of prostitutes; whereas they often bestow their special favours on rakes.

The third harm, which is supposed to be caused by prostitution, is the spread of venereal diseases.

Indeed, sexual intercourse of many men with a small number of women is the primary source of infectious venereal diseases (syphilis, gonorrhoea, chancroid,[15] scabies, phthiriasis).[16] Examination of the girls by doctors is

---

14   Dr. Hammer uses the verb "*lieben*", which can refer to having sexual intercourse: "**Lieben:** mit jmdm. Geschlechtsverkehr haben." Duden, Dudenverlag, 1983, at p. 786.

15   "Chancroid: A soft open sore on the genitals – a venereal disease not related to syphilis – caused by infection with bacteria called Haemophilus ducreyi." A.S. Playfair, *supra*, at p. 49.

16   See: J. Bondeson, "Phthiriasis: the riddle of the lousy disease." *J R Soc Med*, vol. 91, 1998, pp. 328–34.

not suited to promote healthy intercourse since, aside from certain benefits, it promotes a damaging sense of safety that girls supervised by doctors are healthy.

10 Klara Rache

(No. 12 in my files)

26 years old, Protestant, born in wedlock, in a small town in western Prussia. Her father died at 56 from unknown causes. Her mother is still alive.

A 27-year-old brother, a self-employed hairdresser, is married, childless.

A 32-year-old sister is married to a goods inspector, with no living children but three stillborn.

Another sister is married to a carriage owner who had fourteen children. Four are deceased and ten alive (nine girls and a boy).

From six to fourteen, Klara attended *Volksschule*. She never repeated a class. Until fifteen years old, she did the housework in her mother's house. She was then nanny for a year to a hotel owner in her hometown for 60 Marks a year. From 17 to 18 years old, she worked as a parlour maid in a manor house. For the first year she was paid 90 Marks, for the second year 108 Marks. At 19 she lived for six months with an uncle, a master tailor in Berlin, which she enjoyed. The uncle is childless.

Then she worked as a housemaid in Charlottenburg with a rentier for 20 Marks a month. Afterwards she took up a position as saleswoman in Leipziger Strasse[1] for 10 Marks a week. During that time, she lived with her uncle for free. Then she learnt tailoring. Her uncle wanted that to happen because she was engaged to a mechanic. He was employed by an international company in Berlin. For a half year she "studied independently." Then until 26 years old, she worked as a self-employed tailor.

She had three pregnancies from the mechanic. She admitted she also had a few affairs on the side. Two months later she had completely abandoned her profession and was placed under the control of the vice police.

---

1   A main street in the centre of Berlin.

She had lost her virginity to her fiancée, the mechanic, at 21 years old. "My uncle and aunt were away. He stayed with me." For three years she slept with him but "always had a few affairs on the side." Two months after she had abandoned her career, she was placed under vice control.

In these three years, she gave birth three times.

Her first child, a daughter, was born full term when the mother was 21 or 22 years old. The child was delivered by a midwife in Berlin, breastfed by the mother, lived for three weeks, and died from "thrush".[2] The midwife charged 15 Marks for the delivery. The mechanic paid thirty Marks a month child support. "He was very fond of the child. He cried when he heard she was dead."

The second child was a still born infant boy of seven months. The midwife was of the opinion that the infant must have already been dead for eight days. The mechanic also paid the fees for delivery.

The third child, a boy, was also born dead in his seventh month.

The relationship with the mechanic came to an end. He moved to London, where Klara heard in a letter from a friend that he had died. A relationship with a new boyfriend, an officer from a neighbouring garrison town, only lasted a year. "At the same time, she had still had affairs but got no money from the others. They were love affairs."

Then she started at two well-known Berlin dance halls under the same management. She adopted a fancy-sounding name.

"The cloakroom there costed 50 Pfennigs, we stayed on our feet until we left. It was necessary to have a hackney carriage and costume. That cost about 150 Marks. Entertainment and dance were provided there for refined gentlemen. For less than 20 Marks, nobody would agree to leave. 100 Marks were easily taken."

At the same time, she supported "a somewhat idle student doctor from Munich." "He had signed everything,[3] he was to marry me. His mother had thrown him out of his home. I will let him continue his studies. He

---

2   "**Schwämmchen:** A monilia infection in the mouth, producing white patches inside the mouth." A. S. Playfair, *supra*, at p. 233.
3   This may be a reference to a formal engagement contract (*Verlobungsvertrag*).

is still young, 23 years old. He writes me two postcards every day. He is a handsome young man." She will earn money for his studies.

In the dance halls, she got to meet "boot clients" whose fetish is to lick high boots.[4] In addition: "nail clients" who only value well-manicured and beautiful nails. Clients that puncture with needles, or strike with sticks or riding whips, or tread on your back with riding boots or let themselves be trodden upon.[5] Moreover, people who, to put it scientifically, engage in cunnilingus.

A teacher from a Thuringian city often visited. Six months ago, he committed suicide by poison.

He had often visited Berlin, rented a room for 10 Marks a day. Once he sent her 850 Marks.

"I immediately had a butcher's block[6] at home. I am incredibly sensual. Now I have to pleasure myself."

She is also lesbian. Before intercourse, she drinks sparkling wine, bathes, and sprinkles herself with *eau de cologne*.

She intends to continue with her change of lifestyle, perhaps to free herself from vice control, by working for a time. For work, she sees herself as a housemaid or seamstress, living with a married female friend (evidently lesbian) in the west of the city, who had also once made such a lifestyle change. Her handwriting is thin and without pressure.

Assessment: The lengthy celibacy on our ward (which lasted for nearly three months) strongly augmented the girl's sensuality.

Here can be seen a motive for prostitution, which induces a large number of girls not to abandon prostitution, namely the desire to subjugate

---

[4] Examples of boot fetishes are given by Georg Merzbach in *Die krankhafter Erscheinungen des Geschlectssinnes,* Alfred Hödler, 1909, at p. 107.

[5] Merzbach, *ibid,* devotes a chapter to masochism, at pp. 116–74, and to sadism, at pp. 175–274.

[6] Dr. Hammer uses the term *Schlachtbank*. The word is often used in a religious context: "Christus ist wie ein Lämmlein, das zur Schlacht Bank geführet wird." ("Christ is like a lamb that was led to the slaughter." My trans.): Johann Arndts, *Vier Bücher vom Wahren Christenthum*. Evangelischen Bücher-Verein, 1851, at p. 442. The meaning of this sentence is open to interpretation but may be a reference to self-flagellation. On the relationship of masochism and religious martyrdom, see Krafft-Ebing in *Psychopathia Sexualis, supra,* at pp. 10–11.

men. It is a sexual pleasure for many of the girls to watch as reputable men are on their knees before them (Similar to Zola's Nana).[7]

X. Reform Proposals

The reform proposals, which are currently being formulated within a wider group,[8] should in part address the subject of prostitution, and in part transmissible venereal diseases. I will here briefly discuss some of the most important proposals and briefly set out my own viewpoint.

In its present form, I do not consider it be of value to further expand the brothel system. Brothels with examination of men and women, with the protection of prostitutes against professional and age-related risks, brothels with regulations protecting against exploitation by landladies and men who do not pay, are conceivable; yet the introduction of such brothels had never been contemplated by influential parties. The presently existing German brothels do not protect against venereal diseases, but rather all but guarantee that young men will be infected if they make frequent use of them. They do not protect the girls, but rather more or less guarantee that through alcohol they will be physically and mentally ruined, and, apart from food and drink, often earn not a Pfennig.

The controls of the Berlin vice police over prostitutes living independently practically guarantee that both the client and the girl fall ill.

In my opinion, the abolition of the police controls would not lead to any significant increase in venereal diseases. The degree to which procuring should remain a criminal offence, as is now the case, remains to be debated.

The criminalisation of prostitution for men and women is not practicable. I consider that a diminution of venereal diseases and prostitution by these means is improbable. Already 25 percent of persons infected with

---

7   Émile Zola (1840–1902) published the novel *Nana* in 1880.
8   At this time, a group by the name of *Wissentchaftlich-humanitäre Komitee* (WhK), founded in 1897 by Magnus Hirschfeld, met in Berlin, at which Dr. Hammer often attended as guest: Jazbinsek, *supra*, at p. 32.

gonorrhoea are married men according to Neisser.⁹ I saw gonorrhoea rentiers from the health insurance funds visit the hospital with a box of cigars and a bottle of wine. Health insurance members in my experience nearly always are infected with gonorrhoea after payment of a girl. The financially better off men are infected no less and even more than manual workers. Prostitutes are not driven onto the streets by hunger.

There are prostitutes who go hungry and there are those who earn 50 to 100 Marks a day. As conclusive proof that no girl comes under control because she has nothing to eat, I consider it important to note that every girl on her first warning from the vice police already is given a pamphlet with the following content:

1. municipal labour offices (*Arbeitsnachweise*);[10]
2. an excerpt from the poor laws[11] together with addresses of the city shelters, welfare assistance for paupers, and the administrative measures in case of impoverishment;
3. a statement of the proceedings commonly brought against prostitutes;
4. perhaps addresses of relevant foundations.

---

9   A reference to Albert Neisser (1855–1916) who published widely in the field of venereal disease and discovered the causative agent of gonorrhoea that was named after him (*Neisseria gonorrhoeae*). See for a brief introduction to his life and work: Albert Neisser, "On Modern Syphilotherapy with particular reference to Salvarsan." *Bulletin of the History of Medicine*, vol. 16, no. 5, 1944, pp. 469–510, at pp. 469–73. *JSTOR*, <www.jstor.org/stable/44443251>.
10 See: Thomas Buchner, "Arbeitsmärkte Ordnen oder Konstruieren? Öffentliche Arbeitsnachweise in Deutschland (circa 1890 Bis 1914)." *VSWG: Vierteljahrschrift Für Sozial- Und Wirtschaftsgeschichte*, vol. 100, no. 3, 2013, pp. 292–310. *JSTOR*, <www.jstor.org/stable/24548229>.
11 For a history of the legislative treatment of paupers in this period, see: Ernst Knoll, "Die Sozialethischen und Rechtlichen Wandlungen in der Beurteilung des Armenwesens." *Zeitschrift für die Gesamte Staatswissenschaft / Journal of Institutional and Theoretical Economics*, vol. 111, no. 3, 1955, pp. 418–37. *JSTOR*, <www.jstor.org/stable/40747746>.

As regards all legislative measures, it must be demanded that the police operate in accordance, and not in conflict, with the applicable Imperial laws (compare the prohibition of procuring and the brothels permitted by the police in many German cities!).

The bodies responsible for legislating should bear in mind what Bismark said in the Parliament of the North German Confederation on 29 March 1867: "there are many things, that a state can endure — it can ignore them; but it is something else to sanction them by law."[12]

The legislative machine can only work slowly. On the contrary, an individual can quickly adapt their behaviour in a beneficial manner.

The individual man, the individual woman can for themselves abolish prostitution.

Tacitus extolled the emerging Germans, in opposition to the declining Romans, in that for them good morals counted for more than as elsewhere good laws.[13]

As regards education, I consider the first fourteen years of life to be decisive.

Even if punishments and pleasant words are not without some value, a good example remains foremost, and namely from both parents.

It is nearly impossible, to instil children with a moral outlook that is in contradiction with the actions of their parents.

Parents rarely succeed with their children by means of concealment and dissimulation, because children are more acute observers than many parents imagine.

Finally, I must emphasise that in spite of the most careful education a girl can become a prostitute.

---

12   This quote is mentioned by Ludwig Krieger in *Lothar Bucher, die rechte Hand Bismarks. Neue Stenographische Praxis,* no. 8, vol. 1, 1960, pp. 13–18. <www.parlamentsstenografen.de/index.php?option=com_content&view=article&id=129:lothar-bucher-die-rechte-hand-bismarcksq&catid=46&Itemid=170>.

13   Dr. Hammer is probably referring as his source to *Germania* written by Tacitus in c. 98 AD. See: Herbert W. Benario, "Tacitus and the Fall of the Roman Empire." *Historia: Zeitschrift Für Alte Geschichte*, vol. 17, no. 1, 1968, pp. 37–50. *JSTOR*, <www.jstor.org/stable/4435013>.

Glossary

BEZIRKSSCHULE: a primary school located in the local district (*Bezirk*).

BÜRGERSCHULE: primary schools with different curricula and length of school attendance – often divided into lower, middle and higher Bürgerschule.

CONTROL: this is a term used to refer to the control of prostitutes by the Berlin vice police in accordance with the Regulations replicated in Chapter II.

DAMENKNEIPE: a bar managed by a woman.

EDUCATION: Dr. Hammer generally employs *Erziehung* in the context of training for young female prostitutes in the variety of welfare institutions in Berlin at the time. *Unterricht* generally refers to education in the traditional sense either in school or in these institutes. I have tried to retain this distinction between education and training.

FORNICATION: *Unzucht* can have a variety of meanings, but fornication is generally the translation adopted.

FOUNDATION: *Stift* or *Stiftung* refers to one of the wide varieties of charitable, religious, and private foundations operating in Berlin and throughout Prussia.

ELEMENTARSCHULE: generally synonymous with **Volksschule**.

ETHICS: see Moral(s).

GEMEINDESCHULE: primary school in the local area or parish (*Gemeinde*).

GIRL:	Dr. Hammer often uses the word *Mädchen* rather than *Frau* (woman) to describe those he is studying engaged in female prostitution. I have generally translated as girls, but this does not signify any particular age group.[1]
GYMNASIUM:	the highest-ranking secondary school with a nine-year curriculum that conferred the right of admission to university.
HUNGER:	Dr. Hammer often uses *Brotnot* or *Brotmangel* (lack or shortage of bread) to designate lack of food in the context of a motivation to engage in prostitution. I generally translate as hunger unless the context otherwise requires.
INSTITUTION:	I have generally translated *Anstalt* as institution; it is often synonymous with the meaning of establishment in English.
INTERCOURSE:	the German word *Verkehr* or *Liebesverkehr* is generally used by Dr. Hammer to refer to sexual intercourse. *Verkehr* can also signify social intercourse. I have generally translated as sexual intercourse unless the omission of sexual is necessary to avoid misunderstanding.
MAN:	I have generally translated *Herr (Herren)* as man (men), unless the context otherwise requires.
MARK:	the Mark was the official currency in the German Empire from 1871.
MEASURES:	a more general term (*Bestimmungen*) which is also used to refer to **Regulations.**

---

[1] See, for a table providing information on the age at which the girls studied by Dr. Hammer entered prostitution: Jazbinsek, *supra*, at pp. 60–61.

Glossary

MITTELSCHULE:	a category of intermediate schools that included **Bürgerschulen** and **Töchterschule**.
MORAL(S):	Dr. Hammer employs the word *Sittlichkeit* or *Sittlich* which I have translated as morality or morals or ethics or ethical depending on the context. No particular distinction is intended.
PFENNIG:	100 Pfennig = 1 Mark.
PROSTITUTE:	Dr. Hammer employs *Prostitutierte* or *Dirne*. I have translated both these terms as prostitute. Various categories of prostitute are mentioned: *Strassendirne* (street prostitute) and *Kontollmädchen* (female prostitute under police control).
PROSTITUTION:	Dr. Hammer employs a variety of words and expressions for prostitution (*Prostitution, Dirnentum, Dirnenverkehr, Gewerbeunzucht, auf die Strasse, auf den Strich gehen, Körper preisgaben, Preisgabe, käufliche Liebe, für Geld hingeben, das Gewerbe der Unzucht*). I have in general translated all these terms as prostitution.
REFORMATORY:	*Fürsorgeanstalt* is translated as reformatory.
REGULATIONS:	generally used to refer to the police regulations detailed in Chapter II *(polizeiliche Vorschriften)*.
REPEAT:	a feature of the German school system that a child can repeat a class *(sitzen bleiben)* in case of poor performance.
POSITION:	employed to translate *Stelle* rather than the more modern terms, job or employment. See also **Service**.
SELEKTA:	a class for advanced students.

SERVICE:	Dr. Hammer usually employs *Dienst* for what now would be referred to a job or employment, but the word service is generally used here.
SEXUAL INTERCOURSE:	see **Intercourse**.
SHELTER:	the *Städtische Obdach* was emergency housing provided by the Berlin authorities.
TÖCHTERSCHULE:	a category of schools for secondary education of girls, both public and private.
TRAINING:	see **Education**
VOLKSSCHULE:	public primary school often organised according to religious confession, which provided a basic eight years of education from 6 to 14 years old.
WELFARE:	*Fürsorge* is translated as welfare training.
WELFARE FOUNDATION:	*Fürsorgestift* is translated as welfare **foundation**.
WELFARE TRAINING:	*Fürsorgeerziehung* is translated as welfare **training**.
WOMAN:	*Dame* and *Frau* have been translated as woman, unless the context requires otherwise.
YOUNG WOMAN:	*Fräulein* and *Mädchen* have been translated as young woman, unless the context requires otherwise.

Notes on Contributors

STEPHEN CARRUTHERS is a lecturer in the School of Social Sciences, Law, and Education at the Technical University Dublin. His current research interests are in the field of cultural history. Recent publications include "Yilmaz Güney's the Fields of Yuréghir and Arkadaş: From Despair to Hope" in *CINEJ Cinema Journal*, 9(2): 164–192, DOI: doi.org/10.5195/cinej.2021.407; "The Golden Decade of Pornographic Cinema in Paris" in *Academia Letters*, 2021, Article 1781. DOI: doi.org/10.20935/AL1781; and "Hermann Nitsch: 7 Abreaktionsspiel (1970)", Academia Letters (2001), Article 2584. DOI: doi.org/10.20935/AL2584.

JILL SUZANNE SMITH is Associate Professor of German at Bowdoin College in Maine, USA, where she is also an affiliated faculty member in Cinema Studies; Gender, Sexuality, and Women's Studies; and Urban Studies. She is the author of the book *Berlin Coquette: Prostitution and the New German Woman, 1890–1933* (Cornell UP, 2013). Her research and teaching focus on gender and sexuality, Jewish studies, and the city of Berlin from the Wilhelmine era to the present. Smith has published articles in *Feminist German Studies*, the *German Quarterly* and the *Journal of Modern Jewish Studies*, and essays in volumes on *German Women's Writing in the 21st Century* (Camden House, 2015) and *Rebuilding Jewish Life in Germany* (Rutgers UP, 2020). She is currently editing a volume on the cultural history of prostitution in the western world from 1920 to the present and writing a monograph on representations of Weimar Berlin in contemporary German literature and visual culture.

www.ingramcontent.com/pod-product-compliance
Ingram Content Group UK Ltd.
Pitfield, Milton Keynes, MK11 3LW, UK
UKHW021834140426
5217IPUK00021B/1440